# Renovating
# the Soul

# Renovating the Soul

## Meditations on Christ and Life from a Serial Renovator

Andy Parker

**Soul Reno Media**

ISBN 979-8-9908098-0-2 (paperback)

To Diane, Max, Lily, Ella, Molly, and Phin. You are my home.

# CONTENTS

# Introduction

# Lemons and Lemonade

We said good-bye to my mother-in-law (the only family we have left) and our friends whom we love dearly. About five months earlier, while sitting in bed with my wife, I just came out and said it, "I think the Lord is calling me away from pastoral ministry for now." After twelve years of pastoring the church I planted, I was burnt out. I had more years in ministry than I had weeks off in that same time frame, which I had never really considered until things began to take their toll.

On top of the normal responsibilities and stresses of ministry were ample amounts of controversy and conflict, particularly during Covid and the three years that followed. Then experiencing family trauma and tragedy that would break any family, coupled with all the attendant drama that it brought with it within our church I was burnt out...like done.

Of course, this was something I wrestled with for a bit before even bringing it to my wife. She agreed that our family needed time but wanted to make sure it wasn't just a substantial break we needed. We both were determined to pray about it. After a couple weeks, she said she needed a break as well. We prayed about it some more, and then some more after that.

Honestly, we were both scared. But by now, we believed that this is what the Lord wanted for our family and once you come to that conclusion, that the Lord is calling you to do something, you do it. However, I wasn't just going to step down from ministry so that my family could get some much-needed time together to recalibrate our lives. We would also sell everything and move across the country to destinations yet unknown trusting that the Lord would lead the way and bring us where He wanted us.

We prayed much and then prayed more than that, and then we prayed harder than that before bringing it to our children. After praying about it as a family, we all agreed to go on this adventure together. This was a particularly stressful season, as one could imagine, but God in His divine wisdom and grace worked out everything in a way that we will just call miraculous.

We said our good-byes and expended our tears and then it was time to leave the people's Republic of Michigan in the north and move to a deep red state in the deep south. I would be driving the U-Haul (at this point in my life, I hadn't driven anything bigger than our minivan – embarrassing, I know) and my wife would be following behind in our minivan (at this point in our lives, we had never actually driven as a family out of the state before). We were both feeling a bit like Bilbo, being quite a little fellow in a wide world after all.

Oh yeah, I should probably mention that we had to say good-bye to our home as well. Which probably goes without saying, however, this was our dream home that we just finished renovating to meet our family's needs perfectly. One might ask why we would leave it behind? There are a multitude of reasons. Primary among them being that we believed this is what God wanted for our family at this point in our lives. We all needed to hit the reset button and start over in many ways. Also, if I'm being honest, we feared complacency and stagnation. Though challenging in many respects, paradoxically, our lives were comfortable, and comfort makes you soft and weak, and can also make you fearful and less willing to take risks.

We needed to leave everything and go on an adventure. Chris Stapleton's words in "Starting Over" rang true for us. We knew that "nobody wins afraid of losing and the hard roads are the ones worth choosing." We also knew there would be the proverbial river to cross and hills to climb.

I started up the U-Haul, my two sons riding with me as we led the way. My wife was close behind in our minivan with our three daughters, two bulldogs, two guinea pigs and one rabbit. I wasn't super stoked about driving the U-Haul, but I'm still pretty convinced my wife drew the short straw. Like the Autobots, we rolled out to go to our new home that we had only seen some very poor pictures of, to a state where we knew no one, nor had ever been.

This all probably sounds crazy, but in a weird way, made complete sense to us. Why? Because God is awesome and faithful. Sometime before we left, I was outside with one of my daughters looking up at the sky as the sun was just beginning to set, one of our favorite past times. I would always say, "God is an awesome artist," as we looked up at the variations of pinks, oranges, yellows and blues. My daughter asked, "Will the sky be the same where we are going?" I replied, "Yep, and even better than that, God will be." One of the greatest comforts in our lives, regardless of ever-changing circumstances is that God is the same, yesterday, today and forever, which is amazing because He is altogether awesome.

As we drove through many unknown states, I was so thankful to be able to see a small chunk of our country and even more than that, I was thankful to be having this experience with my sons. However, after many hours of driving, and as we began getting closer to our intended destination, I had some thoughts arising in my mind (which is generally a good place for thoughts to arrive). Thoughts like, "You really have no idea where you are going," "You really know nothing about the area except for your brief research online," and, "You just left all of your creaturely comforts, I hope it's worth it." …you know, just some minor, little thoughts.

By God's grace, we finally arrived. Now, it's important to note that we did try to prepare ourselves, at least to the best of our abilities, for the "warmer" climate. Obviously, we knew that the deep south would be warmer than what we were used to. So, we extrapolated from the part to the whole. We've experienced "hot" before, therefore we will just be experiencing more of said hotness…right? However, as I left the U-Haul, my body began involuntarily throwing up water…you may be thinking, "That's funny, he was sweating heavily because it was hot." Nope, you don't get it – I felt like I jumped in a pool and then jumped in it again. I quickly realized this heat was a whole different bird.

As I surveyed my family, I could see that they were also very quickly coming to the same conclusion. By the expressions on their faces, they were all thoroughly convinced that I had taken a wrong turn and that we had stopped, perhaps not in, but certainly just outside Dante's Inferno. It was hot to say the least, and we were not prepared for that. Needless to say, there was a uniform look of concern on all our faces.

I wish I could say that as we entered our new home all our concerns subsided. Let's just say we bought potential. My wife and I love renovating homes. It's an aspect of dominion and there is something awesome and redemptive about the whole process. However, this home was going to need a whole lot more redeeming than what we were originally anticipating, if you know what I'm saying. We knew it would require a lot of work, but we believed the bones of the home to be good.

What we believed to be good bones actually had an advanced case of osteoporosis. If the termites weren't bad enough, we also had foundation issues…like pretty big ones…like parts of our home were more like a skateboard ramp than a nice level surface. Not to mention the house was like an oven, and had been vacant for some time, which means there were an assortment of odors that had been marinating in that oven. Not to be overly dramatic, but this house very well could have been the Devil's fart box for the last several years. Okay, there actually was tons of potential with the house, even though my entire family was wondering why we bought a good-sized property on Mount Mordor.

I'm not going to lie. Internally, I was beginning to question all of my life decisions. Had it been a little cooler in the house and had I been able to find a corner of the house without bugs and cockroaches I may very well have been tempted to curl up in the fetal position while crying and pooping my pants. But since I didn't have access to a clean set of drawers, I figured that really wasn't an option.

But seriously, what do you do in the moment? You're all in at this point. Going back is not an option. You're a man, and not just one who self-identifies as a man, but, you know, an actual man with accompanying anatomy so you can't just go get your therapy hamster. You're also a husband and a father and your family is looking to you to lead. So, what do you do? You step back, you get perspective, you take a deep breath and suck it up and you rally the troops.

You acknowledge the reality of the situation, and you have a family meeting. Yes, it is much hotter than anything we've ever experienced, and yes, we're going to have an adjustment period that may not be very comfortable, but we will adjust. Yes, the house stinks, but we will fix that. Yes, the house is in worse shape than we thought, but that will make the renovation that much more glorious. Yes, the house is a big fat booger, but we are going to make it beautiful. Yes, we have a lot of work in front of us, but we're going to do it together. And, most importantly, it was the Lord that brought us here and He will give us the energy and strength and wisdom and resources we need to fulfill all that He has put before us.

In short, you remember God and who you are in Christ and that He will never leave you nor forsake you, and you remember that

He put you here to have dominion. Or if you will, there is a phrase my wife and I use often, you simply embrace the crazy.

### *How This Book Came to Be*

What you just read was written a couple weeks after we arrived, which by now was some time ago. It almost sounds inspiring right? That was actually going to be an introduction to an entirely different book, but you know, lemons and lemonade and such. It's funny for me to go back through and read that. We were not only ignorant we were pollyannaish in our ignorance.

This was not our first rodeo. We had renovated homes before and lived in every home during renovation. It is always tough at times, but we've grown to love it, well, kind of. We were thinking this renovation would be just like past ones, and we had all kinds of plans as to how we thought things were going to pan out for us. Already burnt out and already terribly broken, we thought we had already learned the lessons we needed to learn. Not so much. As we unplugged from everything, the silence was deafening.

We expected to renovate this home, not expecting that through it, the Lord would be renovating us as well. It didn't take long for things to go from bad to worse and then get worse after that and then after hitting rock bottom to only have the bottom fall out. Needless to say, we thought we were already in the furnace, not realizing that God was going to start blowing on the embers and really heat things up. As Yogi Berra said, "It ain't the heat, it's the humility." And we not only had a piece of humble pie to eat, we had the whole dang thing to fill our bellies with.

As a result, and in the midst of this, I started writing these meditations, thoughts, chapters or whatever you want to call them. Originally, I didn't anticipate that they would amount to anything. In fact, I just started writing as a means of preaching to myself. Honestly, most days I was just trying to hold it together and see

Christ in the midst of the madness, feeling like a kite in a hurricane more often than not.

I don't know that I would ever volunteer to go on this ride again, but I am so thankful that Christ has shown us so much of Himself throughout, and I wouldn't trade that for anything. Again, in classical Yogi Berra fashion we came to a fork in the road, so we took it, and we took the fork less traveled on and that has made all the difference.

### *What This Book is & What I Hope it Does for You*

There are no "how-to's" to be found anywhere in this book. I am not a contractor, or a tradesman, I'm just a tinkerer who tinkers a lot. This book is simply a series of meditations on Christ and life related to our homes and home renovation. Even though life isn't put together with 2x4's many of the principles derived and lessons learned, and reflections given, will apply to a great multitude of areas in your life.

What I hope is that this book will encourage you as you think through everything related to your home. I hope it will help strengthen your marriage as you consider a broader vision for your home and family. I hope that you bravely and fearlessly attack and pursue that vision, whatever that may be for your home and family. As you begin to work on these things, regardless of whatever shape that may take, I hope, more than anything that you are able to see Christ working on you through it all. If you receive any encouragement from this book, I will be well pleased and very thankful.

As you read, I hope you are challenged, and encouraged, and are able to laugh a little bit along the way.

Soli Deo Gloria,
andy

# Chapter One

# Renovation

Amazing grace! How sweet the sound
That saved a wretch like me.
I once was lost, but now I am found,
Was blind, but now I see.

'Twas grace that taught my heart to fear,
And grace my fears relieved.
How precious did that grace appear
The hour I first believed.

Through many dangers, toils and snares
I have already come;
'Tis grace has brought me safe thus far
And grace will lead me home.

The Lord has promised good to me
His word my hope secures;
He will my shield and portion be,
As long as life endures.

Yea, when this flesh and heart shall fail,
And mortal life shall cease,
I shall possess within the veil,
A life of joy and peace.

The earth shall soon dissolve like snow,
The sun forbear to shine;
But God who called me here below,
Will be forever mine.

When we've been there ten thousand years
Bright shining as the sun,
We've no less days to sing God's praise
Than when we've first begun.

I don't need to tell you that those words are from John Newton's, "Amazing Grace." "Amazing Grace" has got to be the most beloved hymn of all time. It doesn't matter what church, what denomination, or what part of the world you're in, when that song is sung on Sunday morning the volume goes up. Even unbelievers will belt out the words of "Amazing Grace," not being fully cognizant of what they are saying. And when these cords start playing at a funeral, it's all over man – everyone is crying.

"Amazing Grace" is such a beloved song because it is describing the most wonderful and most amazing thing, namely what it means to be born again, or if you prefer a theological term, regeneration. In the beginning of John's gospel we read of Christ, "But to all who did receive him, who believed in his name, he gave the right to become children of God, who were born, not of blood nor of the will of the flesh nor of the will of man, but of God." (John 1:12-13).

Before the infamous, and most well-known verse of all time John 3:16, we have this exchange between Nicodemus and Jesus,

Now there was a man of the Pharisees named Nicodemus, a ruler of the Jews. This man came to Jesus by night and said to him, "Rabbi, we know that you are a teacher come from God, for no one can do these signs that you do unless God is with him." Jesus answered him, "Truly, truly, I say to you, unless one is born again he cannot see the kingdom of God." Nicodemus said to him, "How can a man be born when he is old? Can he enter a second time into his mother's womb and be born?" Jesus answered, "Truly, truly, I say to you, unless one is born of water and the Spirit, he cannot enter the kingdom of God. That which is born of the flesh is flesh, and that which is born of the Spirit is spirit. Do not marvel that I said to you, 'You must be born again.' The wind blows where it wishes, and you hear its sound, but you do not know where it comes from or where it goes. So it is with everyone who is born of the Spirit." (John 3:1-8)

"You must be born again." Why? Because there is no spiritual life in us apart from God's regenerating grace. This may sound extreme to some, and well, it is. When our first parents sinned in the Garden, they didn't just fall into sin, their disposition was changed. Still image bearers of God, but now fallen. When they disobeyed God, they essentially put themselves in the judgement seat, trusting themselves over God's word. God said, don't eat or you'll die. Satan said, not so. Instead of crushing Satan right then and right there, man said, "I'll decide." And that is a pretty good rough and ready description of sin.

From that point on, man's will was bent towards self. That is, self-glory and self-exaltation above God's glory. The effects of the fall were total. This doesn't mean that man is as bad as he can be. Never underestimate the power of sinful people to exceed your expectations. However, what it does mean is that the effects of the fall were total. Which is to say, that every aspect of man has been affected, or you could say his disposition was changed. To turn your back on the Author of Life is to court death.

Paul, describing our natural state apart from Christ says this to the Ephesian church,

> And you were dead in the trespasses and sins in which you once walked, following the course of this world, following the prince of the power of the air, the spirit that is now at work in the sons of disobedience— among whom we all once lived in the passions of our flesh, carrying out the desires of the body and the mind, and were by nature children of wrath, like the rest of mankind. But God, being rich in mercy, because of the great love with which he loved us, even when we were dead in our trespasses, made us alive together with Christ—by grace you have been saved— and raised us up with him and seated us with him in the heavenly places in Christ Jesus, so that in the coming ages he might show the immeasurable riches of his grace in kindness toward us in Christ Jesus. For by grace you have been saved through faith. And this is not your own doing; it is the gift of God, not a result of works, so that no one may boast. For we are his workmanship, created in Christ Jesus for good works, which God prepared beforehand, that we should walk in them. (Eph. 2:1-10)

To summarize to the extreme, we can say that to be born again means to be born of the Holy Spirit. Which is to say, to be brought from death to life. The good doctor, Martyn Lloyd-Jones defines regeneration as follows,

> …we define regeneration as the implanting of new life in the soul. That is it in its essence. If you like a definition which is a little more amplified, consider this: it is the act of God by which a principle of new life is implanted in a man and a woman with the result that the governing disposition of the

soul is made holy. And then the actual birth is that which gives evidence of the exercise of this disposition. (Martyn Lloyd-Jones, Great Doctrines of the Bible: Three Volumes in One. Volume Two, p. 77-78)

What happens in regeneration is that the Holy Spirit changes our fundamental disposition. He gives us new life. He changes our heart of stone into a heart of flesh. He enables us to see what God has done for us through Christ. This new life gives us a love for Christ and a desire to live for Christ. As Paul says, we were created in Christ Jesus for good works (Tit. 2:14). He says it this way elsewhere, "Therefore, if anyone is in Christ, he is a new creation. The old has passed away; behold, the new has come." (2 Cor. 5:17).

This is all well and good, in fact, it's not only wonderful it's amazing. However, what does any of this have to do with home renovation? Much and in every way. So much so, that I hope you will never do any work on your home again without first thinking about God's transforming grace in your life.

When it comes to working on our homes we often use the word renovate or renovation. This is a common word in our nomenclature because it is very much *en vogue* to work on our homes today. If fact, there are entire TV networks dedicated to home renovation shows which abound. Not to mention the great multitude of YouTube channels dedicated to home improvement.

However, we do well, to step back and ask ourselves, what does it mean to renovate our home and why do we desire to do that in the first place. For many, it is simply a matter of having their home function better for the needs of their family. While for others, it is nothing more than making something more beautiful. Then there are those who want their home to be a monument of their glory, while keeping up with the Joneses. Like the old saying goes, we buy things we don't need with money we don't have to impress people we don't even like.

12

Although this is true for some, I would still argue that there is a sense in which home renovation can not only be good but can also help us to see more of Christ. The word renovate is derived from the Latin verb *novare*, which means "to make new." When you purchase a home you are bringing new life into that space. You dwell there, and as a result put your mark on it. It becomes an extension, and in many respects a reflection, of you and your family.

When we renovate, we are giving shape, and form and substance to our dwelling. Over the years, my wife and I have lived in several homes. We bought boogers, but they were boogers that we believed could be special, they had just been left for dead. For us, in its purest form, to renovate our home means to bring it to life again. To take that which is dead and make it alive. To take something that is ugly and forgotten and make it beautiful and functional for our family. We find it impossible to work on a home and not see what Christ has done for us and how He continually works on us.

Through the work of Christ, we have been purchased by His blood. We have been redeemed from the slavery of sin and death and have been made alive together with Him. In Christ we are a new creation. And God, by His power and by His grace, sends His Spirit upon us to dwell within us giving us a new heart that loves Christ and desires to live for Christ. Through the indwelling of the Holy Spirit, we are made more like Christ, more useful and more beautiful to God.

I fully realize that we probably won't be singing Amazing Grace as we work on and renovate our homes. Generally, said work and often the problems uncovered therein do not invoke such praise. In fact, sometimes it's just the opposite. However, as we work and we renew and restore, and remove the old and the dead, and make our spaces alive and beautiful again, we should be reminded of Christ's work in us and that should cause us to sing.

# Chapter Two

# A Note to Husbands and Wives

There is a scene in, *The Hobbit: The Desolation of Smaug*, where the Dwarves are about to make their way into, and hopefully through Mirkwood forest. Gandalf has to leave them and go handle some business, but before he does we have this exchange between him and Bilbo. Gandalf, "You've changed, Bilbo Baggins. You're not the same Hobbit as the one who left the Shire…" Bilbo, "I was going to tell you… I found something in the Goblin tunnels." Gandalf, "Found what? What did you find?" Bilbo, "My courage." Gandalf, "Good…well, that's good. You'll need it."

Perhaps you are looking for someone to share in an adventure, or perhaps you are quiet folk and have no use for adventures and think that they are nasty disturbing uncomfortable things. Either way, if you are thinking about taking on a renovation, make no mistake about it, it will be an adventure for which you will be needing to find your courage. And, by God's grace, perhaps you'll find your way back home – there and back again, but if you do you certainly won't be the same as when you left.

There is a saying, "If you want to test your marriage, take on a renovation together." Perhaps this statement is true. Renovating a home can be very stressful especially if you are living in the renovation, and even more so, if that renovation seems to go on in perpetuity. But stress doesn't put anything inside of you that isn't already there. What stress does is enable you to see all the junk coming to the surface. Whatever is inside is coming out. If I were to squeeze a water bottle, it is not surprising that water would come out. Little sinners that we are, when the pressures of life press in on us, we – and others – most certainly our spouse see all that junk we don't want to see.

Not only can renovating your home together be stressful, but it also forces husbands and wives to work in closer proximity together than they ever have. It forces them to make a great multitude of decisions together that they wouldn't be forced to make otherwise. All of this, coupled with the physical labor, discomfort, and mental testing that often ensues on top of all your other responsibilities in work and life and you can easily come to understand the saying, "If you want to test your marriage, take on a renovation together."

Renovating will certainly test your marriage however I do not believe this is a bad thing. Not at all. In fact, I think it's a wonderful thing. Renovating can be like the refiner's fire and your marriage like the gold that it purifies. Marriage is sanctifying, and renovating together will just help get you there faster, amen.

So, yes, renovating your home together can be challenging to say the least, however, I also find it incredibly rewarding. I love working on projects with my wife, and I'm pretty sure that she would mostly say the same thing. For the past twenty years of marriage, we've renovated every home that we have lived in, while living in it. Sometimes, it feels like we've just moved from a mess to a bigger mess (probably because we have). That to say, we've learned a few things along the way. That coupled with years of pastoral ministry,

I might have a tip or two for you to help get you back to the Shire so that you can tell the mighty tale of your adventure together.

This is going to sound totally cliché, and so it is, but it's true. You're a team. Even more than that, you are one flesh in covenant together before the Lord. You are both represented by one family name. This is the closest earthly relationship that you will ever be in. Which means you are both in this together. As you seek to build the other person up you can't help but build yourself up as well. Furthermore, the inverse is also true. If you attack or tear down your spouse, it's not just stupid, it's suicidal.

Many would say that this probably goes without saying, which is exactly why I probably need to stress it all the more. Most people treat their marriage like a competition or an adversarial relationship. How stupid is that? Who wants to live in that environment all the time? Nobody, that's who. And no one in their right mind takes that same approach to any other team they may work on, or with, whether in business or athletics.

If you are working on a team, you want everyone to perform well because you sink or swim together. Therefore, you try to build everybody up and encourage everyone so that you can all perform well and reach your goals. Everyone should be able to understand this. If you enter a team environment and are adversarial and accusatory all the time, you probably won't last long. It's a recipe for disaster, and yet that's how many people treat their marriage, and this often becomes painfully clear in the middle of a stressful renovation.

Many people treat their spouse like they are their enemy, and they are out to get them. This is ridiculously stupid and is a miserable way to live. Probably the one phrase I have repeated more than any other over the years with married couples is this, "Your spouse is not your adversary, they are your advocate." You will never be able to get anything done with an adversarial attitude, and if you do you won't be happy.

Your spouse does not exist to thwart everything that you want to do in life. A way to fight against this toxic attitude is to remind yourself that you are a sinner. You are quick to speak, quick to rush to judgment, quick to condemn other people, and quick to excuse and exalt yourself. As sinners we are quick to give ourselves the benefit of the doubt and assume that we are the only ones in the world that see things clearly, while at the same time believing everyone else to be deaf, dumb, blind, and stupid.

If you begin with these basic presuppositions, you do well. I am a sinner in much need of grace. I should be slower to speak and quicker to listen, and a good chunk of the time I should probably just shut up. I'm not God, therefore I am not all-knowing, nor all-powerful, nor am I all-competent. Gaining wisdom is cool, and the only way to get there is through humility.

Beginning with a spirit of humility and grace eagerly desiring to learn more about the other person as you work together is awesome. One of the reasons why people are so tested when they work together on renovations isn't because of what's exposed in the other person it's what's exposed in themselves and they don't like it, so they blame the other person. Any time you play the blame game you're an idiot. Kill your ego, take responsibility, and in seeking to make everybody and everything around you better, starting with your spouse and family you'll be built up too. Also, no wife wants to live with a drill sergeant, so don't be a jerk. And no husband wants to live with an over-bearing mother, so don't be a nag. Being patient and kind with one another goes a long way, coupled with lots and lots of repentance.

Also, just to state the obvious again, marriage means you are in a one-flesh union with your spouse. The two become one, which means your home should be a reflection of that. This means that the same roles and rules apply. There is the old expression that the guy builds the house, and the gal makes it a home. There is a lot of truth to this, but the reason I illustrate this is because if you really want to build a household where everyone is flourishing you are going to have to do it together and communicate, and like, I mean a lot. You are going to have to share yourselves with one another, and in doing so become one with a common vision for your home.

If husbands want their wives to flourish in the home, then they are going to have to do everything in their power to make that happen. You can't expect someone to make a delicious cake without first giving them the raw materials to make it happen. And wives, in baking said cake, first make sure it is something that your husband cares to eat.

Make sure to listen to your spouse. If something is important to them it is most likely layered in ways that they may be unaware of, and if it's very important to them, it's usually multi-layered. We all have different perceptions and experiences and have drawn different conclusions regarding things. For example, when naming your children, there is always that one name that you can never name your child because of that one person who ruined it for you. We can do the same thing with colors and styles and whole houses regarding negative and positive associations and often not even realize it. Being loving, humble and reflective goes a long way to finding common ground where you both can be constructively creative.

Lastly, again this should go without saying so let me say it. Have fun and remember to laugh a lot and mostly at yourself. You are going to make mistakes along the way. We have a saying in our house, "No education is free." Meaning any lesson you learn comes at a price. Just remind yourself that no matter how expensive the lesson was it's still cheaper than college and most likely more fruitful. As you learn and grow together, you will learn and grow together – put that on a cat poster – Boom! Remember, you began to renovate because you wanted something in your life to function better or be more beautiful or both. You will never reach your destination if you reach it alone. It is always marriage and family first…you can put that on a cat poster too!

# Chapter Three

# Dominion

E veryone has a vision for their home. What's yours? We all
have a way we want our home to look. The question is
whether we are shaping our space in order to fit that vision. Are we
shaping and forming and molding and making and ordering our
homes to fit the lives we desire, or are we being shaped and
constrained and limited by them? To use an agricultural metaphor,
are you tending and cultivating your garden, reaping all the benefits
therein, or has it become overgrown and filled with weeds?

What do you envision your home to be? Is it simply a place
where you lay your head? Is it just a dwelling you provide for your
family – just doing your duty. Is it a place filled with warm memories
or is it a place that is so sterile it resembles a hospital. Is it a museum,
or a showroom? Is your home a place where you spend most of
your time, or is it a place where you are barely at? What about
location? Are you in the city, or the suburbs, or the country? Is this
by choice?

Many people just buy a home and that's it. Now, contentment
is one thing, we should all be content. However, contentment

should never imply lack of ambition or vision for your household and what it can be. And when I say household, I am not just talking about your dwelling. I am talking about the people that fill it and all that they can be, and how your home can be used to help shape and order that vision. Therefore, I would argue that if you only see your home as a common dwelling space for family members, it is not as though your vision is far too small for your home, but also for your lives.

Some may argue that working on your home or spending time thinking over such things is materialistic and self-indulgent and the like. I think this is misguided and silly. The clothes we adorn ourselves with can certainly be materialistic and self-indulgent, but this doesn't keep us from wearing clothes. And this doesn't keep us from wanting to communicate things about ourselves with our clothing, that much is unavoidable. The question is whether or not what is being communicated is appropriate and fitting as far as function within your life and work.

I would argue that working on your home and desiring to do so is a good thing. I would even go further than this. Shaping and ordering your home, making it function well, and making it beautiful is not just being constructive with our time and making our living spaces more pleasant. No, no, no there is much more to it than that. In fact, I would argue that this gets at our very nature as image bearers of God.

In short, man was created to have dominion. What does it mean to have dominion? In order to answer this question, we have to go back to the very beginning. What man is, is determinative on what he does. These are probably familiar verses to most, but helpful to see again here,

> Then God said, "Let us make man in our image, after our likeness. And let them have dominion over the fish of the sea and over the birds of the heavens and over the livestock and over all the earth and over every creeping thing that creeps on

the earth." So God created man in his own image, in the image of God he created him; male and female he created them. And God blessed them. And God said to them, "Be fruitful and multiply and fill the earth and subdue it and have dominion over the fish of the sea and over the birds of the heavens and over every living thing that moves on the earth." (Gen. 1:26-28)

In their book, *It's Good to Be a Man*, Michael Foster and Bnonn Tennant, summarize dominion as follows, "The reason that God creates man on the earth, according to Genesis, is for productive, representative rulership. This is what it means to exercise dominion: to fruitfully order the world in God's stead." (19).

God had just created paradise and man was to put his mark on it…I don't know about you but when my kids were young the most terrifying thing for me to do was let them in a room I just recently refinished…but God doesn't do that. He says, shape this world, mark this world, fill this world, protect this world, order this world for my glory.

God places man in Eden, a place where God would dwell with man, a temple sanctuary, and tells him to get to work, and to get after it. From the very beginning man was to work on, give shape to and order his space. Man fell into sin and was cast out of the Garden paradise sanctuary. Though fallen into sin, he is still an image bearer of God, and he still seeks to fill, order, create and give shape to his dwelling and surroundings. The cultural mandate is hard post-fall, not partaken of without sweat and toil, but it is not abrogated.

God's people were given a visual reminder of who they were and what they were made for, as well as who He is and how they would be able to enter into His presence once again through the blood of atonement brought into the most holy place in the tabernacle and later the temple. Both of which were beautiful pictures, re-creations of the imagery of Eden.

When Jesus, the second member of the Triune God took on flesh and dwelt among His people, He achieved our righteousness and bore our sins in His body on the tree that we might die to sin and live to righteousness. By His wounds we are healed (1 Pet. 2:24). The blood of Jesus speaks a better word, an eternal word, a word of mercy to those who seek refuge in Him. He makes atonement for His people once and for all and upon His ascension He sat at the right hand of the Majesty on High.

The temple was destroyed. God's dwelling is now with man through Christ and the outpouring of His Holy Spirit. In Christ, we are the new temple, with Jesus Himself being the Cornerstone. Jesus has all dominion, rule, and authority. He is shaping, remaking, renewing, reordering, and renovating if you will, all things to His glory through His people. He is making a fit dwelling for them. This begins in the soul, yes, but is not isolated there. This renovation bleeds out into all of creation. We are to put Christ's mark on everything we do.

Fruitfully ordering the world for God's glory is dominion. Obviously, this is not exclusive to our homes, but it most certainly begins there, and will give shape to our lives in very much the same way that worship should shape our lives. Worship changes us from the inside out drawing us further up and further in, seeing and knowing and savoring more of Christ. As we see and know and savor, it shapes and orders us. As we are shaped and ordered, we then give shape and order to everything around us. We order our spaces to reflect who we are and what's important to us.

So, when we are talking about dominion in our homes we are not just talking about finishes and the number of bathrooms and the like, but rather this is a dominion that begins with your life before the Lord. As your life is rightly ordered to the Lord, it will have a corresponding impact on every area of your life. This is not exclusive to the home, but it begins there.

Does your home reflect who you are and your vision for your lives? Does your home enable your family to function the way that you want given the stage of life that you are in? Does it best enable fruitfulness and productivity? Is it a beautiful place? If not, then you should go get busy molding it and shaping it and ordering it into that. This is pleasing to the Lord.

None of this requires you to have a super fancy home that looks like it's ready for photos in a home magazine, you might be happier if it doesn't. What this means is that you are to take what the Lord has given you in time, talents, and treasure and make the most of it - ordering it accordingly, to His glory and the vision that you have for your home and family, and children and grandchildren, all the way down. Take what He has given you, magnifying it, multiplying it and manipulating it to better fit your life. And then, make it all beautiful.

This doesn't mean that you need to spend a bunch of money on a renovation. But it does mean that you should use the resources that you have to order and beautify your home accordingly. This is an aspect of dominion, and this is good.

# Chapter Four

# Household

W hat comes into your mind when you hear the word, household? What do you instantly think of? For many of us, we simply equate the word household with dwelling, and maybe with family. However, most would probably prefer the seemingly warmer word "home" over household. After all, home is where the heart is.

The word household, and all that stands behind it is even a much bigger word than that of family, though it includes it, and dwelling, though a family is typically centralized somewhere. The household is an institution and economy. In fact, it is the institution on which all other institutions are to be built.

Before one could rightly understand what a household is, they would need to understand what a family is, which means they would then have to understand what marriage is. However, that's not all, because what stands behind a proper understanding of marriage is a proper understanding of what it means to be a man and a woman.

Therefore, the household is founded on a man and a woman entering into a covenant for life before the Lord. But a proper understanding of masculinity and femininity enables us to understand the roles that both are to play and contribute within that marriage, which also further defines their roles as father and mother.

So then, as the two come together in a one flesh union for life, the man comes into the marriage on mission and his wife is now on sub-mission. That is, her role is subordinate to, but enables the fulfilling of the mission. This marriage grows into a family and into a covenant household, that household being a living organism, an entity, an institution if you will with a shared vision and mission.

This is much, much different than your home being where the heart is or it being a place where you lay your head, or as I saw on a plaque the other day, "Home is the place where you're most comfortable pooping" – I didn't buy the plaque, but I thought about it. With this in mind, one can begin to see the generational impact of just one faithful and fruitful marriage. Carry this out a couple generations and you cannot only see God's blessings generationally given, but you can also see how a household as an institution becomes the most foundational building block for a fruitful civilization.

The Biblical household which was once seen as the necessary foundation for all of society and its flourishing is now outrightly disdained. The reasons for this are legion and beyond our scope here. What is important here, for our purposes, is that we define our terms so that we know exactly what our objectives are regarding the "home." What exactly are we talking about? Most would think this question is unnecessary because we all just intuitively know what we are talking about.

However, how we answer these questions, and define our terms determines the purpose behind what we are doing. Namely, what are we trying to build? What are we renovating and what's the objective, what's the end? If you are thinking in terms of just creating an awesome space or making something pretty, that is considerably different than sitting down and saying this is what we want our lives to look like, and this is what we want to build generationally. So, yes, what fills the home is the central focus, namely the family, but we are looking at cultivating gifts and abilities within the family covenantally and then extending that further up and in, to a thousand generations.

I had this conversation with my children the other day. I said, your mother and I have five children, a fact of which they are very aware, but then I asked them what it would look like if they all had five children of their own and we all continued to live in the same general area. And then, multiply that out a couple generations, with each successive generation looking to build and create and expand and bless. It doesn't take long before you go, "Wow, that's pretty awesome." When you get to that point, you're just starting to get the idea of how God desires to bless His people generationally. You're just beginning to understand how big and awesome the Biblical concept of the household is.

When you're looking at building or renovating, you are looking at best conforming your dwelling to that vision. You are asking, how can we best facilitate all that God has for us here? You begin with the end in mind, and then conform to that, not the other way around. If so, you can still create awesome and beautiful spaces, but in the end, they will simply be whitewashed tombs, or if you will, Ozymandias' ruins.

When my wife and I think about our home, we try to think of the much broader category of household. Because of this, we think of our home as the home-base for all operations. How does this home best facilitate the functioning of our lives, and how can we centralize as much of that as we can, regarding work and school and everything that fires out from that like homesteading and the like.

As a family, you determine all the things that are important to you. Then you determine how to build and renovate spaces to best facilitate that. If you can do that where you're at, wonderful. If you can't, well then, get busy figuring it out. I know the idea of moving or renovating sounds overwhelming and costly to most. However, you have to ask yourself, is it more costly not too?

Unfortunately, most of us only think in terms of what we could potentially lose, or rather in this case, how much discomfort we will have to endure, instead of thinking in terms of what we can gain. Remember, your home should be a means to an end not the end itself. This should put every renovation in perspective and help you to prioritize what gets renovated and when.

Understanding the Biblical ideal for the household isn't just important when thinking in terms of our individual homes. Even more than that, it enables us to understand what God has designed for His church in the world. Paul says of the church, that we are,

> …members of the household of God, built on the foundation of the apostles and prophets, Christ Jesus himself being the cornerstone, in whom the whole structure, being joined together, grows into a holy temple in the Lord. In him you also are being built together into a dwelling place for God by the Spirit. (Eph. 2:19-22)

God's people have a place where they physically meet, however, the vision of God's household is much bigger and grander than a simple dwelling. It is very much the same way for your household.

You may be like me in that your family tree looks more like a ravaged bush than an oak. Which is to say it's a hot mess all the way down and all the way through and you have no experiential knowledge to pull from. Or it could be that your home simply isn't what you know the Lord would have it to be. The prospect of trying to build a Godly legacy or bring reform to your home seems like an impossible task.

Nothing is impossible with God. He brings healing, and direction, and strength and peace. You have to trust in Him and His promises to bless your home. But you can't get anywhere if you don't start somewhere. So, no matter where you're at today, come to Jesus. What are some small things you can start with today that would be a pleasing aroma to the Lord and a stench to the world. Do that, and then do it again, and don't stop.

When we think of the term household, we should not just think of warm sentimental feelings or feelings of joy, acceptance, deep love, and creativity. We should also think of expansion, and conquest, and victory because a Godly household is the greatest threat to a sin ravaged world.

# Chapter Five

# Family

Everyone knows that it is all about family. No, I am not talking about the theme of every *Fast and Furious* movie, though each one of them is a cinematic masterpiece, and it is unheard of that those films would be robbed by the Motion Picture Academy ten times. I am actually talking about real life and real families. Now, the super holy rollers, and overly pious among us may scoff at that statement and quickly point out that the chief end of man is to glorify God, and to enjoy Him forever. This is true and praise God for that, although the sanctimonious buttholes among us usually don't seem to ever be enjoying much.

So yes, we are to glorify God and we are to enjoy God, but where and how does that happen? In worship? Yeah, absolutely and I hope so. But is our glorifying of God and our enjoyment of God exclusive to an hour or two on Sunday mornings? Of course not. One may then be tempted to answer by saying that this also happens on Sunday evening and throughout the week at all of our church activities as well. This is a common misconception but a misconception, nonetheless.

God intends for us to glorify Him and to enjoy Him with all of our lives and I would argue that fountain head begins in the home. All of this begins with one man and one woman becoming one flesh in covenant for life walking before the Lord. This covenant is the structure and safe haven around their procreation and their multiplication in the world. They reproduce, and it is through the reproduction of Godly offspring that the earth is filled with God's glory. Little image bearers raised in the fear and nurture of the Lord.

The home is ground zero for it all. The home is the place where we learn about authority and submission. The home is where we learn what a father and mother are and how they are to interact with one another as husband and wife. The home is our first school, our first sanctuary where we learn to worship and love the Lord, and the first place where we discover and exercise our gifts and abilities. The home is the first place where culture is made that gives shape to all other cultures. The home should be a place bustling with activity and creativity and instruction and discovery and laughter and joy and maybe some more laughter.

The home is ground zero for all of life. A healthy God-fearing church is always downstream from healthy God-fearing families. In fact, many of the metaphors for the church come from the home. God is our heavenly Father. The church is the household of God. Christ is our elder brother. Through the blood of Christ we are brothers and sisters in the Lord and so on.

Now, I am not minimizing the role of the church and worship in the world, not at all. Worship is the Red Bull that gives us wings to attack everything in the world for the glory of God and perhaps and hopefully with a little gusto. However, the family is foundational to all of it. By God's grace, Godly marriages make Godly families that make up a Godly home, that over time becomes a Godly household. This then, is what makes up the church and society.

Often, regarding any type of home renovation, we either want to make something pretty that is ugly, or just make something function because whatever it is, it is just creating challenges for the operations of lives. However, this is to only fix externals. It is true, to fix those things will make your home more picture worthy for an Instagram post or will make it function better as to make your home more productive in some ways, but to focus on these things without first building up what fills the home, that which matters most, is to whitewash a tomb.

We've all been guilty of this. That is, thinking that if we just change this thing externally that will have an equal and opposite effect on the relationships in our home internally. Another thing that we often do, which is driven by the same impulse, is that we look at people with beautiful homes and just assume they have beautiful lives. I can tell you, without a degree of hesitation, that some of the people that seem to have it all together, are the most messed up. Of course, this is not true across the board, however, what this illustrates is that we need to be careful what standard we use to measure our homes against.

Wanting to create, wanting to build, wanting to renovate, and wanting to make the things around us beautifully functional or functionally beautiful can all be great things. However, fundamental to any of those things are the answers to these questions, "What is a home, or rather what is a family that is to fill it?" Many people desire these things that are dominion related to a home without ever asking why they desire those things in the first place, or what those desires are meant to create and build and shape and order. To what end do you strive? To what end are you looking to build and/or renovate?

Again, I do not think those desires are bad things in and of themselves. However, I do think many, if not most, have a very short sighted, deficient, and profoundly unfruitful view of the home because it is disconnected from building and continually maintaining that which matters most. Perhaps it's a cliché saying, but its cliché in the best of ways, "A home is only home because of the ones who fill it."

We can never lose sight of this. First, because this should not only ground our homes in love but also in principle. Second, it should help give us perspective that not all beautiful homes are truly beautiful. They may be gorgeous in a photo, but upon closer inspection you discover they are fake fruit wonderfully displayed in a wooden bowl, or fake flowers in a beautiful vase. They may look splendid, especially in a photo, but there is no life there.

If you really want a beautiful home fill it with children to love and pour into. The best way to love them is to give them a father and a mother who love each other and love the Lord. We should be constantly asking ourselves, "Are we building, restoring, renovating that is, working on and building up the relationships that matter most to us?"

Our children and grandchildren and great grandchildren and so on will outlive anything that we have worked on. Our great grandchildren could care less whether or not our home was show worthy. There is absolutely nothing you can do to your home that will have a greater impact on them than the type of home you have. Is it a home filled with a love for and fear of the Lord? Is it a home filled with grace and forgiveness and prayer? Is it a home where all can flourish and grow and take risks and make mistakes? Is it a home filled with creativity and joy and learning? Is it a home filled with life? Our legacies are not brick and mortar, but people. This is a love that flows throughout generations.

Therefore, any building, any renovating begins in the soul and then should flow outward beginning with your marriage and your children. In this respect, your home becomes a reflection of the Lord's work on you. This is really the only way for your labors to have fruitfulness and longevity. Are we maintaining, are we building up that which matters most? What are we teaching our children about our homes? Do they know what matters most? Are you teaching them to think generationally? Do they know what the end is, what the vision is? Do they know how any work you may or may not do fits within that vision? Include them in this whole process. Share your heart with them and be honest with them.

If you are reading this and it sounds great, but also discouraging, because you come from a long line of brokenness I get it. I truly do. My family tree looks more like a withered, half dead, trampled-on bush. I didn't have any examples and I didn't have any role models and I didn't have the proverbial coach or mentor to show me how to be a good husband and father.

I won't lie to you. Any changes you want to make in your life will be hard work. There is no renovation without cost, and this applies to every area of your life. However, one thing I know for certain is that God takes us where we are at and brings us to where He desires us to be. He draws straight with crooked lines, and He is good and faithful and true and lovely and beautiful. Through Christ, He is pouring into His family and making, renovating a home fit for His family.

You can't get going if you don't start where you're at. The renovation begins today, and it begins with you, and those you love most. So come and welcome to Jesus Christ.

# Chapter Six

# Legacy

What are you living for? Or maybe a better question is, what are you willing to die for? Weighty questions, I know. Most, in answering these questions would be quick to answer, with something stock that would make them look super pious and virtuous. Most in the church, at least of the remotely orthodox kind when asked, would probably say, "The glory of God" to either of the above questions. Of course, a cursory look at their life would lead you to conclude that they are full of… "You know, you know the thing."

What are you giving your life to, and why? What are you sacrificing for, and why? What are you willing to die for, and why? Again, weighty questions I know, but they are important to visit and revisit from time to time, and then to honestly reflect upon. Does your life reflect the way that you just answered those questions? If not, why not? What is out of whack and how do you get it back on track, or just on track to begin with? What really matters to you and why, and is that of any eternal, or even earthly significance whatsoever?

The way you answer these questions should guide and govern your life, which also informs us how you will be remembered after you're gone, which is inevitable. In watching home shows I have noticed a trend that is often expressed through people's desire to renovate their home. They will say things like, they are investing in this renovation because they want this to be their forever home.

This is a place where they want to raise their children, or have their children return to for family gatherings with the grandchildren. They want their home to be a nice place to facilitate that and to make all the memories that will accompany this ingathering, which is a wonderful sentiment that most can relate to. Or they want to build something nice to leave behind to their children. Again, also a wonderful sentiment, and a godly one. We should want to leave behind an inheritance for our children and not just our children but our children's children's children. But it is important for us to stop and ask what it is that we are actually leaving behind.

Look, despite what a pain in the butt it is at times, I have loved working on our homes with my wife over the years. I don't have any memories in those homes that don't involve my wife and kids. And I can't think of any of those memories that couldn't have been had in another home. Over the years, my wife and I have never bought our forever home. Honestly, I don't even know what that's supposed to mean. We've bought homes that we thought were ugly ducklings, but that had the potential to be swans. If we thought we could sell for a profit and move to a home that would allow us to potentially repeat this process, and better facilitate our life in that home, then we did it.

Although this has been a tremendous amount of work, certainly not stress free, it's enabled us to survive financially in ministry over the years. We've been able to do this several times now and God has blessed our work, and we are thankful for that. I am proud of the homes we've worked on, but there isn't anything that we have done in any of those homes that will last.

# Legacy

I don't care what materials you use, or how expensive they may be, or even if they were forged in the fiery hot flames of Mordor those materials will break down over time. There is simply no project or renovation you will do that, given a long enough timeline, will not need to be redone at some point, regardless of the craftsmanship or materials. I don't care how timeless you think your design is, at some point it's going out of style. Granted, it may come back around and be vintage at some point, but then you will have to redo it anyway, because things wear out over time.

I can't tell you how much forever crap I have ripped out of kitchens and bathrooms, all seemingly heavier than the last, or perhaps it's because I'm older than the last. Living through renovations makes you age in dog-years after all. The home we are in now was built as a forever home for a doctor. He used all high-end materials, but that was thirty-five years ago, and all those materials are just straight up nasty now. They are either rotting, breaking, or fading, and honestly, I can only take so much peach and pink and mauve in my life. Needless to say, as of writing this, I have almost removed all that from my life, with the exception of some smoker yellow walls, my Scarface tub & jacuzzi and my pink toilet. I am still on the fence about my pink toilet.

My point in saying all of this is that the stuff that really matters, the forever stuff, is not the stuff that fills our homes but rather the stuff behind the stuff. This doesn't mean that we shouldn't work on our homes and desire to make them awesome places of work and creativity and rest and so on, where super awesome memories are made. Memories of feasting and laughing, and memories of building and tearing down, and so on. Praise God for all of it. However, what this does do is help us to put things into their proper perspective, which should help us to keep the main thing the main thing.

I think renovating homes is an aspect of having dominion. Bringing back to life something that was left for dead or making something ugly beautiful, or just creating something new is fantastic.

But all of these things, and all of the works of our hands are a means to an end, not the end itself. The real and only lasting legacy that we leave behind is the people we pour into, beginning in our homes with our children. Any renovation should better allow for that, while at the same time not be confused with that.

There is an old saying, "All things in life will soon but pass, only what's done for Christ will last." Of course, this is true, however, we ought not spiritualize this saying to the ninth degree, thus becoming an overly pious jerk. God created man to have dominion over this earth and to put his mark all over it for His glory. Jesus took on flesh to redeem man and restore creation. The work of our hands matters and is important, but in the end all stored up earthly treasures are going to be destroyed by moths and rust and what not. The heavenly treasures are of the kind that endure. It is important that we see our homes as a blessing from God and as a means for storing up one type of treasure, while not being the treasure itself. In the end, this distinction makes all the difference in the world.

# Chapter Seven

# Fragrance

Here is a thought you've probably never had before. Have you ever wondered what Eden smelled like? What was the fragrance of Eden? It is impossible to know, but I bet it was awesome. Everything was new and fresh and beautiful and perfect. Everything in bloom without any defilement in the air. God doesn't just make things that are visually beautiful, but sensationally wonderful across the board. If you could think of the most perfect memory you have, you may not remember the fragrance that filled the air, but I bet if you smelled that fragrance again you would immediately be taken back to that place with all the memories and all of the emotions.

However, East of Eden not everything smells like Eden. It seems that for every well pleasing aroma there is an equal and opposite stink. If I said warm apple pie you would probably intuitively smile. Even if you don't like apple pie, you would probably still smile because of everything associated with it. But then if I said, pile of manure, you most likely would not smile, in fact, I dare say that there would be a correspondingly opposite effect.

The fact of the matter is that fragrance is something that we are ever conscious of but very rarely give much thought to. This is also true of our homes. Of course, of the two options we would prefer that the aroma of our home is pleasant over the alternative, but it is generally not something that we give much thought to. In his book, *Reforming Marriage*, Doug Wilson asks the following questions, "How would you describe the spiritual aroma of your home? When visitors arrive, before virtually anything is said or done, what is one of the first things they notice about your family? In many cases, it is the aroma. Do they feel as though a bad attitude crawled under your refrigerator and died? Or do they think someone has been baking spiritual bread in the kitchen all afternoon?" (9).

Eden was God's dwelling place with man on earth. The Garden being the most holy place in the beginning, because that's where God manifested His presence most fully before man. Though God is omnipresent, and we know that heaven is His throne and earth is His footstool and He is not isolated or restricted to any one area, He does reveal Himself more fully and manifest His presence more fully in particular places that He has designated. In popular parlance, and without any degree of irreverence we could say that this was His home, of which, the tabernacle and later the temple would come to represent.

When the year begins, we usually begin it with gusto, which usually translates into some form of Bible reading plan for the year. For most, they are a little tired after getting through the end of Exodus, but when they hit Leviticus they begin to feel like Alice tumbling down the rabbit hole. The book of Leviticus has shipwrecked many a poor soul. However, if you were to keep reading you would discover a book filled with aromas.

Think of the alter with all the meat and fat continually being offered, and all the bread and grain offerings, and the incense and the oils. The tabernacle would have been a place filled with aromas. Everyone who was close to the tabernacle would have associated all those aromas, all those fragrances with the house of God. Just as we have word associations, both positive and negative, we also have scent associations as well.

Just think of Christmas time. I love Christmas time for a great multitude of reasons. Even just mentioning Christmas conjures up a whole litany of memories, and images and aromas. Cinnamon and peppermint and gingerbread and cloves and pine. The scent of all those Christmas cookies that are only baked this time of year filling the whole house. All of those aromas remind us of time with family and all of the joy contained therein, with all of the accompanying feelings and emotions.

This happens with design as well, and I think this lies behind much of the recent desire of many to buy an old farmhouse, or at least decorate their homes as such. We live in a crazy, fast paced, unstable world. For all our interconnectedness today, most still feel completely disconnected from themselves and from their past. There is something about an old farmhouse. It seems stable and enduring, housing a multitude of generations. Even if we're not rooted to our past this home seems to give us that.

When we think of a farmhouse, we think of something stable, organic, peaceful; something that is rooted and grounded. We think of family and generations, land and livestock, hard work and a simple kind of life. We also think of fresh baked bread and apple pie. The aroma of something, the fragrance of something that is layered and isn't exclusive to its mere scent.

Just one more example. When I was a kid, I remember being dragged to church. Apparently, it was a place where we were supposed to be that everyone hated. There is a lot to unpack there, far beyond the scope of this book. It was an old church with maroon pews that smelled musty and old. Needless to say, the fragrance that accompanies old church buildings was not tops on my list of favorite odors. Fast forward several decades and I found myself pastoring in a musty smelling old church building with none other than maroon pews. I grew to love that smell not particularly because it was the most pleasant odor in the world, but because I associated it with all the life and the people that I loved that filled that building.

Paul says this in 2 Corinthians 2:14-17,

> But thanks be to God, who in Christ always leads us in triumphal procession, and through us spreads the fragrance of the knowledge of him everywhere. For we are the aroma of Christ to God among those who are being saved and among those who are perishing, to one a fragrance from death to death, to the other a fragrance from life to life. Who is sufficient for these things? For we are not, like so many, peddlers of God's word, but as men of sincerity, as commissioned by God, in the sight of God we speak in Christ.

Through repentance and faith in Christ, we are God's house spreading the fragrance of the knowledge of Him everywhere. Does the aroma of Christ fill your home? The aroma of joy and forgiveness. The aroma of hope and healing. The aroma of hard work and creativity. The aroma of learning and laughter...and maybe a little more laughter. What is the aroma of our home? What is the fragrance that we are left with? What do people smell when they enter our home?

We've bought some homes that stink, some worse than others. One home we bought had a nice pile of dog crap waiting for us on the living room carpet. Another left a nice loaf baking in the toilet for us – that was a nice first impression. The latest home we bought didn't have any poop waiting for us, perhaps because it wasn't necessary due to the amount of rot and water damage that marinated the whole house with a pungent aroma. All that to say, I am very sensitive towards the scent of our home. Nobody wants to have the stinky house, which is something that I am paranoid about, so I usually have wax warmers going everywhere.

However, as we take possession and begin to fill these stinky houses with life and love and laughter, and also blood and sweat and tears, coupled with lots of new materials, not only do the scents that fill the home begin to change but so too the aroma of the home. And here is the thing, this is not something that you can fake. Everyone can tell the difference between a fresh baked apple pie and an apple pie air freshener. There is a difference between the real-deal and that which is artificial.

All of this is true in our homes as well. Whatever renovations, or changes we may make, they will be nothing but air freshener unless we are also pouring into those that fill our homes, while at the same time seeking to bring our lives into greater conformity to Christ's. This is a well-pleasing aroma to the Lord, and this is an aroma that should not only fill our homes but the whole earth.

# Chapter Eight

# It's What Fills the Home that Matters

People want nice homes, and there is a huge market for home stuff. There are endless amounts of home décor stores. When I was a kid, I remember seeing a bunch of mom-and-pop hardware stores and maybe a couple of big department stores that also sold home related things. But now, there are major hardware retail chains and home décor stores everywhere. Not to mention the endless amount of home renovation shows. Actually, there are whole networks dedicated to this genre of show. Then there is YouTube, with its endless supply of do-it-yourself channels, coupled with the myriads upon myriads of channels dedicated to home related things: decorating, home making, baking, organizing, and on and on and on. All this to say that people are into their homes.

I think all this can be a really good thing as far as it goes. Just from a creational standpoint, I think this is all an aspect of dominion and that's great. God is a great Designer, Artist, Architect, Builder, and Restorer. Man was made in His image and His likeness, and as all children do, we mimic and imitate our Father. We have an innate desire to create and renovate and restore and make beautiful. Given the wonders of capitalism, we have this ever-burgeoning market. Supply and demand after all.

Given all of this, one would be tempted to draw the conclusion that everything home related was doing just as well. What I mean by this, is that, if people are spending this much time and energy and money working on their homes and beautifying their homes, then there should be an equal amount of work and beautifying going into the people that fill their homes. Which is to say, that even if we reduced the home to a mere dwelling, which it's not, but let's just say that it is for a minute, we would have to ask ourselves, a dwelling for what? Well, for a family. All that time and energy and money is going into this home for a reason. Therefore, families must be doing very well.

This is kind of like assuming, that just because we spend billions every year on public education we must have an educated public. With that amount of time and energy and money going into education we must be doing pretty well, right? Like I said…kind of like that. You can dump all the resources in the world at something and you are just flushing your money down the toilet if you don't know what target you're aiming at, or what foundation you're building on, or what standard you're conforming to.

The general assumption in all of this is that people know what the home, or if you prefer a more Biblical word, household is for, or rather what it is. Most people would look at you like you're an idiot just for asking that question. It seems so basic, why even ask. The underlining working assumption, in the most generic sense, is that the home is a dwelling for people that care about each other. Which is the equivalent of saying education is about learning stuff. This may be true but really tells us nothing.

This just shows you how messed up we are culturally, or how far down the greased slide we've slid. When thinking of the home, the vast majority of people aren't thinking of covenant and marriage, and children, and the economy of this family with a shared mission and vision and so on.

It should be interesting to us and shouldn't go unnoticed that there seems to be a troubling trend between people investing in their home while at the same time everything represented by the home is being culturally crapped all over. Divorce is now commonplace, and that's assuming that people are still getting married. There is an ever-growing number of adults just shacking up and playing house. We now call that cohabitation – which sounds pleasant, doesn't it? Like two bears occupying the same cave. Marriage is mocked, patriarchy is disdained, feminism is exalted, masculinity is considered toxic, children are murdered in the womb, and if they are brought into the world they are sent off to the state as quickly as possible to be "educated" by a transgender mermaid.

All of this, while at the same time Americans are spending billions of dollars on their homes. This is a classic case of whitewashing a tomb. The container is beautiful, but it's holding death. We think that if we gussy up the one, then it will bring life to the other, or will at least give the appearance of life on social media, but it doesn't work that way. All the king's horses and all the king's men aren't putting Humpty Dumpty back together.

You can fix everything around your home, but that won't fix your family and make it a home. You can have the coolest kitchen in the world, but that won't teach your girls how to be homemakers nor will it make fellowship sweet. You can have the coolest workshop there is, but that won't teach your kids how to swing a hammer or change the oil in their car. You can have the most beautiful finishes in the world and that won't make your home full of life and love and joy.

I love working on my home and I can understand why the market is growing, but I also think there is a lot more going on here. I think this is a classic "If you build it, they will come" scenario. That is, if you can just fix all the externals, then everything else will be fine. If you fix what's broken here, then it will fix what's broken there. It doesn't work that way. In fact, the door swings in the exact opposite direction.

If you want a home that is pleasing to the Lord and a sweet-smelling aroma to the Lord then you have to begin by living a life that is in pursuit of Him, by cultivating a marriage that is in pursuit of Him, by raising children that are in pursuit of Him. We are God's renovation project. As He works on us, that is a work that works outward. It is the lives that fill the home that matter most. This is what we want to build up. Just to be brutally honest, your children won't give a damn about the finishes you used in your home, nor will they care about the type of flooring you decided upon. They care about whether you got down on the floor to play with them.

Not only that, but we can spend a ton of time, and energy and money renovating our homes to make them nice for our families while at the same time neglecting the people we are trying to bless. I am not saying that we shouldn't work on our homes. What I am saying is that all renovation begins in the soul first. What does the Lord want from you? What does the Lord want from your marriage? What does the Lord want from your children? Dominion begins here and then works outward, not visa-versa.

The secret to any renovation project is knowing what's broken, or ugly and how to fix it. This is where we all begin. With the realization and profession that we are all broken before the Lord. That we are rebels, that we are selfish, that we are lawbreakers and sinners, that our real problem is not cosmetic, but that our foundation is bad, and that we are dead and in need of resurrection. When we come to terms with this reality and call out for Christ, the great renovation project begins, and there is nothing so messed up that He cannot fix.

Through Christ, our homes should be places of repentance and forgiveness. Places filled with grace and mercy, and love and laughter and joy. Places bursting at the seams with activity and creativity. In short, we want our homes to be places that are overflowing with life. Therefore, any work that we do on our homes should help to facilitate that in our homes. At the end of the day, it is the life that is filling our homes that matters most.

# Chapter Nine

# You're a Full Gut Job

The first words I usually utter when we enter into a new home are, "Wow, this is going to be a lot more work than I thought." I think the first words I uttered as we walked through our current home after taking possession were, "Wow, this is a much bigger mess than we thought." Those were the words that came out of my mouth. I won't share the ones that were swirling in my head. Those ones were a bit more colorful. Like a Skittles color palette, and I was tasting the rainbow, straight up 100-proof.

Anyone that has done any type of renovation knows there are cosmetic renovations. These are usually called "refreshes." These are fun because you get to see immediate change. They are also much less expensive and take less time, unless you're Rockefeller or a designer that doesn't live in the real world and thinks that spending money on the most expensive finishes increases the value of a home at a corresponding rate. So, there are the refreshes and the facelifts and then there are the real renovations.

These are like opening Pandora's Box that unleashes untold curses and troubles upon mankind. Okay, maybe I am being a little dramatic. My point is, that whenever you get behind the walls you see what's really going on. What you thought was sound and solid often is not. When you start pulling those walls back you find out where all the corners were cut.

You are able to see poor plumbing and electrical. You are able to see where there is rot and water damage and hopefully where it's coming from. You are able to see the mold and perhaps, termites or the remnants of the colonies that have since moved on. You are able to see any structural issues and bad framing. You are also able to see any foundation issues. These are budget killers and stress inducers, but they have to be addressed. They are no fun and, on the surface, provide no immediate visual reward.

Here is the thing though. If you don't change the stuff behind the stuff, then all of the new stuff that you put on top of the old stuff, might look pretty for a time, but it's really just lipstick on a pig, or if you will, perfume on a turd. This is why most people would like to simply remain "blissfully ignorant" regarding everything that is going on behind the walls, telling themselves that it's probably fine. And now that everything looks fine on the surface it is confirmation that, in fact, everything is indeed fine.

The interesting thing is, if you asked people what type of renovation their lives most reflect, they would say cosmetic. Most people, even in the church, believe that they are basically good people. They would even say this much, "I am a good person." And given that they are a good person and have just declared their goodness, they know that they should also be humble, so they follow up their declaration of goodness with a, "but." But what? "I am a good person, but there are certainly some areas I can improve in." What this really amounts to is what we will call spiritual Michael Jordan syndrome. Even though he was the greatest, he could still improve on certain areas of his game.

We secretly think that we are not perfect, but pretty dang close. And because we are striving towards perfection, or so we tell ourselves, while at the same time excelling in humility, we will admit that we could improve our game. After all, we are not the best at every single aspect of the game. You get the point. We pretty much think we're awesome but are willing to admit that we could be even more awesome. The awesome that we can add to our preexisting awesome is always an external awesome. This is basically the doctrine of man, in every religion and non-religion religion outside of Christianity.

The fact of the matter is, we are far worse off than we can possibly know and, in Christ, far better off than we can possibly imagine. There are really only two men as far as the Bible is concerned, Adam and Christ, and all men are under the headship of one or the other. In the beginning God created all things and they were all very good. Man was created in the image of God, to rule and reign over creation, representing what God was like to creation.

Adam sinned choosing his will over God's, thus seeking to be on the judgment seat determining good from evil. As Adam fell into sin so did all his progeny under him. Adam being the covenant head represents us all. All men are born under Adam's headship. All are born with his fallen nature. This fallen nature runs all the way down and all the way through. This doesn't mean that we are all as bad as we can be. It does mean, however, that every aspect of our nature was infected and affected by sin and by rebellion.

After the fall, we all still bear God's image. However, now it is perverted, distorted, corrupted, and bent towards self-glory. This is one reason why we think we are all naturally pretty awesome, or that our thinking and doing should be the standard for all thinking and doing, and that somehow the "universe" should conform to our will. Which means that we are usually more than willing to admit areas in ourselves where we can improve upon, but don't want anyone tinkering around behind the walls because we know in our heart of hearts that our life is really a house of cards. If someone starts really looking around and digging stuff up the whole thing will come crumbling down, so we suppress this truth in unrighteousness.

However, Jesus, the last Adam and our New Covenant Head, ushers in a new humanity. He is the great renovator and restorer of our souls. The thing is, through the redemption that He accomplishes for us, He doesn't just return us to a creational glory. He makes us better, transforming us from one degree of glory to another, which will culminate in His return, and the renewing of all things, where He will dwell with man in new heavens and new earth, at which time man will be unable to sin.

Christ was without sin, though born in the likeness of sinful flesh, He was not born with the corrupted nature of Adam. He was without corruption. He lived the perfect life that we could not live and was obedient where all other men failed, even to the point of death, death on a cross. As the New Covenant Head, He represents us in His death, and He represents us in His resurrection. This means that through repentance and faith in Christ, we are a new creation. The Christian life then is becoming more and more of what we already are in Christ.

All this to say, that Christ changes the entire infrastructure of the house. He is the solid Rock, everything else is sinking sand. Because we are a new creation in Christ, with a new nature, we want the rest of our lives to reflect that. The old man has passed away, behold the new has come. Paul says it this way to the church in Colossae:

> Put on then, as God's chosen ones, holy and beloved, compassionate hearts, kindness, humility, meekness, and patience, bearing with one another and, if one has a complaint against another, forgiving each other; as the Lord has forgiven you, so you also must forgive. And above all these put on love, which binds everything together in perfect harmony. And let the peace of Christ rule in your hearts, to which indeed you were called in one body. And be thankful. Let the word of Christ dwell in you richly, teaching and admonishing one another in all wisdom, singing psalms and hymns and spiritual

songs, with thankfulness in your hearts to God. And whatever you do, in word or deed, do everything in the name of the Lord Jesus, giving thanks to God the Father through him. (Colossians 3:12-17)

Until we get to the point where we can say, "Wow, I am a much bigger mess than I ever thought," and admit to ourselves that we are naturally a full gut job, any attempt to work on our lives will be lipstick on a pig, or if you prefer a more Biblical metaphor, a whitewashed tomb. Because Jesus has already done all the heavy lifting, we get to participate with Him in the beautification process.

# Chapter Ten

# Water Damage

I hate water. Okay, I don't really hate water, I love it because it's necessary for our survival and stuff, so there is that. But I hate water. That is, when it is in my home where it is not supposed to be. In the house that we are currently living in, there is water damage everywhere. Leaky windowsills, leaky door sills, leaky roof, leaky refrigerator, leaky hot water heaters and a leaky dishwasher. Just a little bit of water leaking here and there in just a handful of little spots over a long period of time creates so much damage.

Nobody wants water in their home, we go out of our way to waterproof everything: roof, basement, showers and so on. If there is a way in, water will find it. If there is a crack in your foundation, a crack in your caulk, or a crack in your grout, water will find it. When most of us think about water damage to a home, we usually think of the big things like water flooding a basement or a pipe breaking and unleashing a pool of water and so on. We think of large amounts of water coming in all at once causing all kinds of damage. Of course, no one wants that. However, in my experience it's not the big things that get you. It is the slow steady leak that goes undetected. It is the constant, steady drip that you don't think is a threat.

We think, "It's just a small thing; it's just a very little amount of water, how much damage can actually be done?" Most of the time, when looking around windows or doors you can't even see any holes or cracks where water could be getting in. It's usually something that your eyes don't even catch, something you are probably not even aware of. This is why it's usually the little foxes that get into your vineyard repeatedly over time that destroy your harvest.

The thing that always hurts the worst with this kind of damage is all the extemporaneous damage. This kind of water damage always spreads. We just replaced our side door. The sill of the door was rotten, but that wasn't the only place where the damage was. Therefore, it wasn't like we could just replace the door and be on our merry little way. Not only was the sill rotten, but also two layers of subfloor underneath the sill. Fortunately, when I ripped out the subfloor the joists were still fine.

However, this was not the case with a leaky window in our bedroom. This was probably a leak that went on for some time, perhaps ever since the house was built thirty-five years ago. Because of this, the damage is extensive. It's not just two layers of subfloor that are rotten (so much so that you can step through the floor with minimal effort), but also some 2x10 sill plates and the framing all around the window. An itty-bitty little leak over a long period caused a tremendous amount of damage.

It's not just that the water damage spreads, that's bad enough. It's also what that water damage brings, namely mold, rot, and termites. Not to mention the fact that it just makes your home stink. If these things get detected early on, no harm no foul. You do everything in your power to seal things up and dry things out. However, when things persist undetected, the water will rot the integrity of the wood and everything around it. The only solution then is to remove everything that is rotten, replace it, and then reseal everything up again, and then hope that the problem is solved.

Every time I see the effects of water damage anywhere, I always think, this is the perfect visual for all the "little" sins we tolerate in our life. Often times they go undetected but the effects on our soul are a constant steady drip that is just slowly rotting everything away. Just as was the case with the water damage, all of this sin has an impact on everything around it as well. It is a rot that loves to slowly work its way outward.

In my experience in ministry over the years, I can tell you this is where most of the danger lies. This is not to say that we shouldn't be on guard against the "big" things. It is to say, that it is almost always the little things that add up or lead to the big things. Nobody wakes up one morning and says, "You know what? I want to shipwreck my faith today." Nobody wakes up and says, "You know what? I want to commit adultery. I want to become a drunkard. I want to become addicted to porn. I want to ruin my marriage. I want to embezzle money from my employer."

These are not things that just happen. People don't just fall into these things. The vast majority of the time it was a slow, steady drip that caused a tremendous amount of damage. The author of Hebrews says this, "Therefore we must pay much closer attention to what we have heard, lest we drift away from it." (Heb. 2:1). A slow drift over a long period of time takes you far away from the harbor, and without any navigational tools it's impossible to find your way back. This is why we are constantly warned to be watchful.

The sins we begin to tolerate become accepted and then they become normal. Sin has a callousing effect on the soul. Callouses don't just spring up overnight. They develop over extended periods of time through constant use. Sin dulls, desensitizes, numbs, and progressively hardens the soul. Psalm 1 paints a vivid picture of this hardening effect:

> Blessed is the man who walks not in the counsel of the wicked, nor stands in the way of sinners, nor sits in the seat of scoffers; but his delight is in the law of the LORD, and on his law he

meditates day and night. He is like a tree planted by streams of water that yields its fruit in its season, and its leaf does not wither. In all that he does, he prospers. The wicked are not so, but are like chaff that the wind drives away. Therefore the wicked will not stand in the judgment, nor sinners in the congregation of the righteous; for the LORD knows the way of the righteous, but the way of the wicked will perish. (Psalm 1:1-6)

The walking leads to standing and the standing leads to sitting. The way to prevent all of this is to delight in the law of the Lord and meditate on it day and night. If you are brutally honest with yourself, you need to reflect upon these areas of your life. You know they are there. You've just chosen to ignore them because you think it's a little leak, it's just a little water damage, but nothing serious. After all, it doesn't rain all the time, right? Drip, drip, drip, drip, drip, drip…

Tolerance will lead to acceptance, that will ultimately lead to approval. Where do you need to repent? Where do you need to make changes? Where do you need to sure things up in your life? It is usually the things that you don't think are a big deal that will turn out to be the biggest deal over the long run. And here is the thing, at least with the water damage you can see the extemporaneous damage that is done, but with sin it is impossible to calculate the effect that rot has had on everything around us. On our relationships, on our productivity, on our performance, and so on. Repentance will most certainly make your life better than it is.

The beauty in all of this is that Jesus is the great Renovator of our souls. There is no damage so bad that He cannot fix. There is no amount of rot that He cannot restore. There is nothing broken that He cannot rebuild. To see in all of the shadows and nooks and crannies of our lives, so that we can identify where the cracks and separations are, we just need some Light. Praise God for Jesus.

# Chapter Eleven

# It's Ugly Before It's Pretty

There are a lot of rewarding aspects to renovating your home. It is rewarding to take something ugly and make it pretty. It is rewarding to work with your hands. It is rewarding to fix problems and create spaces that function considerably better for your family. It is rewarding to be creative and acquire new skills. It is also extremely rewarding to finish a project. To remember what it was and then be able to see what it now is…we'll just call this manifesting a vision – that sounds cool.

However, renovation projects can be hard and can test you in a great number of ways, exhausting resources and every ounce of mental energy you have. Renovations can get even harder when you are living in the thick of them. Part of the reason for this is that it is hard being surrounded by a mess which is seemingly impossible to contain. Possibly the hardest aspect of living through a home renovation, especially if you are the one doing all the work, is that everything gets worse before it gets better.

You feel like you are pouring out all your resources, you are exhausted, and you can't get away from all of these projects staring you in the face. You look around at the work of your hands and think, "Wow, this really looks like crap!" All this pain, all this sacrifice, and all this suffering (okay, maybe I'm being a little dramatic) and all you have to show for it is more of a mess than you started with.

Along with my wife and five children, we spent three weeks demoing our current house, filling four thirty-yard dumpsters while it was about 105 degrees, which was awesome. I dropped fifteen pounds in three weeks. I am thinking about starting a weight loss channel on YouTube called moving crap from A to B, which I am sure would be a hit.

I remember looking at our house after a few grueling weeks and saying to my wife, "How can it look even uglier than it did three weeks ago? It looks even worse now." We have a saying in our home that we use often, "It's ugly before it's pretty." In this case when we ripped out what simply looked to be old and dated, which we thought would only grant cosmetic updates (a wall moved here and there, with a bathroom inserted here, and a laundry room moved there and so on), suddenly became a much bigger project.

As we ripped everything back we could see how bad everything actually was. We discovered all the problems: structural issues, rotten subfloor, leaky windows, and our little termite friends that had been feasting on the joists under the master bedroom, which created a cool half-pipe to skate on. "It's ugly before it's pretty" isn't just something we say as a coping mechanism, though it's certainly that. We say it because it's true and because we need to be reminded of it all the time. When you really start smashing away at things, you get to see what things are really made of. You get to see where all the problems are hiding. The problems were all there before, but now you can see them and get to work on them.

What seems to be a much bigger mess really is not, in the grand scheme of things, and is actually the necessary beginning to any renovation. You haven't created any new problems you've just revealed all the nasty. Is that hard? Yep. Is that inconvenient? Yep.

Is that uncomfortable? You bet. Is that necessary? Absolutely, so much so that without it you are really just putting lipstick on a pig.

Truth be told we are a bunch of snowflakes. And when I say we, I have three fingers pointing right back in my direction. The reason I know that I am way softer than I care to admit is because of the ease at which I get frustrated when something doesn't go the way I want it to. I think every project I take on should be easier than I think, less expensive than I think, and take less time than I think. Is that too much to ask? Apparently so…because I'm entitled to nothing.

When things get uglier, we don't know how to handle it. We think this can't be right, and that things should be getting better not worse. And of course, it is getting better, but not in the way that we anticipated. We live in such a whitewashed, glossed over, manufactured, social media world. We don't really want to see all the ugly, so when we do it is shocking to our souls, and we don't know how to cope. Most just cover it back up and pretend like nothing ever happened as they reach for their therapy hamster.

However, until we rip everything apart and can be brutally honest about the ugly, things are never really going to get pretty. I think this is a principle that applies to all areas of life, but most certainly to our walk with Christ. Unfortunately, today the only thing that evangelicals seem to be excelling at is their ability to whitewash everything. I would even go so far as to say the entitlement mentality, that is so corrosive to our culture, has been perfected in the church with the world actually getting her cues *from* the church and not visa-versa.

I don't know where this idea came from, that Christians are somehow entitled to a life of ease and comfort. I have baptized many people, who thought, "This is no fun," after their baptism because things in their life got seemingly harder and uglier. Of course it didn't, not really anyway. When Christ moves in, He turns on the lights, tears everything up and rearranges all the furniture.

Which is to say, you see all the junk and it sucks; it's uncomfortable, and in many respects is no fun.

This doesn't ever really change, though admittedly, there are periods in our lives that are much more jarring than others. We call that growth. Repentance usually isn't easy because we naturally love the taste of sin and have to train our palate to hate it. It's a constant battle, like a seemingly endless demo in the worst heat and stink imaginable. You get to the end of all the hard work and progress that you thought you were making and think, "What the heck, man…this sucks! I feel like I'm further behind than when I began." The fact of the matter is, Aslan has to cut away all those layers of dragon skin that we've gotten accustomed to, and rather fond of wearing.

Job's sufferings were not immediately removed. Jonah still had to go to Nineveh. Saul really did try to kill David. David's own son tried to stage a coup and one of his sons raped one of his daughters. Did I mention that David was a man after God's own heart. Daniel was delivered from the lion's den but was still stuck in Babylon. Paul was tormented by his thorn in the flesh, which wasn't taken away, and then he died a violent death by having his head cut off. Not to mention all of the disciples were violently murdered, with the exception of John, but that wasn't for a lack of effort.

I say all of this not to discourage you, but rather encourage you. As we unearth all kinds of junk, spiritually and literally, and God seems far away, it is those times when He is often the closest because it's His light that reveals and ultimately removes all of the junk and all of the nasty. It gets uglier before it gets pretty. We have to come to terms with the ugly, so that we can see beyond it to what is truly beautiful.

# Chapter Twelve

# Work

In our culture we don't much like the word work. It has a negative connotation. We jokingly say that work is a four-letter word. Which of course it is, however, the intent in saying this is to mark this word out with other notorious four-letter words that will have to go unmentioned. The idea is that work is to be set aside in our lexicon with other unmentionables. We call them curse words.

When we do talk about work it's usually something of a necessary evil. Dolly sang about working "9 to 5," and Lover Boy reminded us that we are just "Working for the Weekend." I'm totally dating myself, but you get the point. Work is something that we are forced into, but it's not really something that we want to do and it's certainly not something that we find joy, or meaning in. This is very stupid and has contributed to a destructive culture of entitlement and envy that is rotten and ruinous.

Wanting the fruit of labor without laboring is not the way that God designed the world. God Himself gave us the pattern of work and rest in the beginning. With God Himself working six days and then beholding the work of His hands and rejoicing in His creation as very good. We are wired to work and then rest, to create and then reflect and rejoice. To desire to circumvent this process is not only unwise, but stupid. The work not only enables us to rejoice in the end product or the completion of a task, but when work is seen in its proper light it holds the keys of its own reward. Work is, in and of itself, a blessing and nothing good comes without it.

It is true that after the fall of mankind into sin, work is hard. But even here God is good. Hard work teaches us much about God and much about ourselves. And though we may have perverted the created order we have not changed it. God, in His grace, still rewards our labors. There is the old saying that you get out of life what you put into it. This is very much true. Another way of saying this is that you will reap the fruit of the seeds you have sown. No fruit is reaped without first laboring to sow those seeds, and that doesn't happen without sweaty brows and calloused hands.

When my wife and I got married we wanted to have a "nice" home. We both grew up in broken homes and our family trees look more like trampled on bushes, and neither one of us grew up "having things." We weren't even really sure what a "nice" home was, but we wanted it to be pleasant, welcoming, and warm- a space we loved to be in and would be ground zero for our life together.

Neither one of us had money or skills, and when it came to home renovations neither one of us knew anything about anything, and that's not me being hyperbolic. What we did have was a will to work, a willingness to look stupid while doing so, and a commitment to one another. Oh yeah, we purchased our first home before YouTube, in fact we didn't even have dial up the first year we were married. All this to say there was a lot of trial and error.

All this required work- usually much more than we anticipated. This was often uncomfortable for the both of us, and more often than not was very frustrating and humbling. We have both eaten our fair share of humble pie along the way. In all our pie eating, we've come to understand that the best thing you can do is to keep working, keep moving forward, and not stop. There seems to come a point in every project where things are harder than you thought, more expensive than you thought, and you are confronted with more unknowns than you thought you would be. At this point you want to curl up in the fetal position and quit. This is the sweet spot we call growing pains, and the only way to grow is to work through it.

As we continued to work on our homes and the Lord continued to work on us, the desires that we had for our home changed. As we've developed a bigger understanding of what a Biblical household is to be and do in the world, what we wanted out of our home matured. How does this best facilitate the work that the Lord has called us to and what we desire for our home and family? How will this function better and how can we make this look pretty? These are questions that we are continually asking ourselves.

We've owned several homes now, each one being a much bigger project than the last, and each one requiring more work than the last. As a result, each one has forced us to grow more than the last. None of this growth would have happened had we been afraid to put in the work, afraid to learn and be uncomfortable, or afraid of looking stupid.

And when I'm talking about growth, I'm not just talking about growing in skills, of which there is still much growth to be had, I am talking about growing as a people, of which there is still much growth to be had. Here are a couple life lessons for you. None of the growth you want out of life is going to happen without hard work, sacrifice and pain. Amen. Also, all of life is work that never ends. Also, amen. This isn't bad, it's preparatory for the next trial and life. Which means, in many respects we are constantly striving, constantly pressing forward, constantly renovating and constantly working.

I asked one of our daughters the other day what her thoughts were on our most recent move. I asked because I was interested in how she was processing all of it. The home turned out to be much more work, or a much bigger dump than we originally anticipated so there has been an awful lot to process.

She told me she was thankful for the move and how multitudinously hard it's been. Not that my daughter isn't absolutely amazing, but I was a bit surprised to get this answer from a teenage girl, so I asked why. She said it was because she now knows she is capable of a lot more than she was before and was thankful that she has grown as a person as a result. It was amazing to hear my daughter understand how overcoming hardship and doing hard work is good for the soul.

Our life in Christ is one great big fat renovation that requires constant work. Don't get me wrong. I am not saying that we contribute to being positionally in Christ. That is, that we contribute to our salvation in any way. This is entirely a work of God, planned by the Father, purchased by the Son, and procured by the Spirit. We contribute no more to our regeneration than we did to our generation. We have been saved by grace through faith and this is all of God, and not our own doing.

We are not saved by good works, however, we are saved to good works. Despite what some glossy teethed pastor may tell you, this is a lot of work. When we purchased the home we're in now, we bought it with cash. It's ours, bought and paid for in full. However, to make it a fit dwelling for our family there is a tremendous amount of renovating work that needs to be done.

When you repent and believe in Jesus Christ, you are a new creation, bought and paid for by His blood. You belong to Him, and His Spirit resides in you. However, when He moves in, the renovation begins. But here is the thing, once in Christ, you are now part of that renovation. Repenting of sin and growing in righteousness is challenging and often frustrating and is usually far more work than we think it will be. This is where and how you grow, through work, through labor, through sacrifice.

Paul says it this way to the church in Philippi, "Therefore, my beloved, as you have always obeyed, so now, not only as in my presence but much more in my absence, work out your own salvation with fear and trembling, for it is God who works in you, both to will and to work for his good pleasure." (Philippians 2:12-13). And then he goes on to say in v.14, "Do all things without grumbling," which is hilarious in many respects because we so need to hear that. "Okay, we'll work, but we won't be happy about it." No! We should be happy about all of it because of what it is producing in us.

His work in us and on us never stops. He is bringing us further up and further in and is transforming us from one degree of glory to another. He is renovating our souls making us more beautiful and more functional for more of His work.

# Chapter Thirteen

# Rest

Confession time, I suck at taking breaks. It's true. After every time I take a bit of a break, or a rest, I always think, "Wow, I really needed that." Which you would think this would inspire me to be more conscious regarding future rest. However, I am a bit of a glutton for punishment. I love work and I love projects, and even more than that I love completing projects. I have a great number of expressions that communicate this in my home. "Nothing feels as good as a finished project." "I'll get rest when I'm done." "The only thing that removes stress is completion." "Nothing succeeds like success." Or the ever popular, "I'll rest when I'm dead."

So, yeah, I suck at rest. However, not only is work a creational mandate but so too is rest. God baked rest into the creational cake. We need it. We are not God, and sleep and rest are a great reminder of that. Having a theological discussion on the nature of the Sabbath usually leads to some manner of debate regarding what we can and can't do, when we can and can't do it, and so on, and is far beyond the scope of this book. Some people are wired so tightly regarding this that if they sat on a piece of coal, a diamond would shoot out of their butt. They love the Sabbath so much they want everyone else to be miserable one day a week with them.

The last thing in the world we want to be is a sanctimonious butthole, the world has enough of those, however, God did bake into the cake a "six day and one" pattern of work and rest. I say that here to simply remind us that we are designed for rest. We need it. We need it not just for worship, but also for a physical and mental rest, refresh and recalibration as well. Not only did God bake rest into the weekly cake, but we also see that His people and their land were given special festivals, rest days and weeks marking out and remembering God's redemptive work in history. The people of God and their land were also given a special year of Jubilee every forty-ninth year.

All this to say, that despite all the sanctimonious "buttholery," rest is very important and baked into the creational cake and is only neglected at one's own risk. This is a very important principle to remember when renovating your own home, especially if you're living in it during renovation. If you're living in your own renovation this can be a horrible stressor because you are surrounded by work. The entirety of your life is in a state of upheaval. Everywhere you turn there is work to be done. Everywhere you turn there is a mess. Everywhere you turn you are stepping over something. When everything feels like it is in a state of chaos, your life can feel like it is chaotic.

Having lived through renovations before as a family we knew they could be stressful, but everyone pulls together, sacrifices, works hard, completes the work and the end is always very rewarding. However, our current home was a much bigger renovation than we anticipated and as soon as we moved in it became a demolition free-for-all. My kids jumped right into demo, ripping apart their rooms because they were disgusted by them. This left me feeling very proud, so proud in fact, that I didn't stop to consider that everything all at once was, well…a hot mess. It was totally worth it to watch all my kids swing some hammers and smash some stuff up. However, eventually the dust settled, as it always does.

As the dust settled, well, mostly settled, we found ourselves in some inconvenient living arrangements. Our family of seven was all living in and sleeping in our master bedroom, which was also tore up, but it was the best room in the house and was mostly tolerable. There was no other room, apart from the master bedroom, for the kids to go to have their space, either to just play or have some time to read or whatever. Because, again, everything was tore up, like badly. Everywhere you looked there was work, lots and lots of work. Work upon work... everywhere... always all at once... work.

In order to remediate any of the current situation that we found ourselves in we were going to have to work our way out of it. What do you do? You start working and hammering your way through projects and rooms. None of the work is going to finish itself, so you just have to get after it. No whining, no fussing, just work. But there was no stop to the work. We would make progress in one room only to find more problems in another room. Or we would complete one project and feel good about ourselves, but then look around at all the work in front of us and become completely demoralized and begin questioning the meaning of life.

Again, what do you do? You work more and you work harder. You get after it, and you get it done. The problem is, you can only keep up a certain level of intensity and focus for so long before things start to fall between the cracks. Your work starts to become counterproductive, or projects begin to take twice as long because they are the last thing in the world you want to do. When the candle is lit and burning at both ends you can get a lot of light, but the candle will burn out faster.

Even on Sundays, if you take the day off from any labor around the home, you are still living in and marinating in work. Which, just FYI, is not restful. Burnout is a very real thing in work, in life and in renovations. I know this for certain because in one of our homes the previous owners were done. They started to renovate and were tired, burnt out and wanted out. We were able to buy the house at what we believed to be a wonderful deal, because desperation is never a good place to be when selling. It worked out well for us but not so much for them. Had they stayed the course perhaps the story would have been different. So, you never want to get into a state where you are so tired and so burnt out that you hate your home.

There comes a point when you have to unplug and get away from it, and you have to learn to trust your spouse. My wife is much better at knowing when the family needs a break than I do. Getting away from it all, even if it's just for a short time or a day trip, can help give perspective. Work is like crack, and I'm an addict, and if I'm around it, I'm smoking it if you know what I'm saying.

The mess isn't going anywhere, but your children will be, and sooner than you think. If you keep plodding away, the work will all get done, but it's not all getting done in a day. Things will all get done, but it will take time, and if you are like me you have an uncanny ability to continually underestimate how long a project will take. I can't tell you how many times I started working on something and told my wife that it would only take a minute or two, only to find myself working on the same project eight hours later.

As a man, it is much harder for me to walk away from a project than it is to bury myself in one. It's not a bad thing to love work. However, it is a bad thing to never get away from your work. Rest reminds us that we are not God. Rest enables us to refresh, reload and recalibrate so that when we get back at it we are more efficient and more effective at our work. Even Jesus needed to get away and have quiet time with His Father. If it was necessary for Him it is most certainly necessary for you and I as well.

# Chapter Fourteen

# Reality

We live in an age of reality TV. Well, at least we call it that anyway. Or perhaps more telling, we live in an age where even our "reality" TV is manufactured and scripted. In fact, there is a whole genre of reality TV that my wife and I simply call, "home shows." These are typically shows where a residential home renovation is chronicled. A designer and general contractor are followed from start to finish through a project, which can be as simple as renovating a bathroom, kitchen, or bedroom, or all of the above.

My wife and I love these shows, some being noticeably better than others, but it's really the only TV we watch, so we usually end up watching them all. It never ceases to amaze us how some social worker and a social media influencer can afford to spend $800,000 or something ridiculous like that on a home and renovation. Anyway, we like watching these shows for a multitude of reasons. Primary among them, we like watching something being restored and being brought back to life. We enjoy seeing something that has been abused or abandoned being made beautiful and functional again.

We also like watching for inspiration. There are some amazingly talented people out there and it's awesome to watch them work. Sometimes we watch for education, occasionally picking up new tricks along the way. And sometimes we watch in judgment, "Why did they do that? We would never spend that! That is hideous! Why didn't they address this, that or the other?" You do it too, don't judge me.

These shows, almost all of them, operate on the same script. We are introduced to a nice couple and what they need renovated in their home. We are given the budget, again leaving me to ask what in the world these people do for a living, and then we're given the plan and can see how beautiful it's going to be in the end, usually through some computer-generated images. All of the stuff is moved out, and the renovation begins. At some point along the way, drama is injected into the episode, usually with some unforeseen problem arising, leading most sensible people to ask, "How on God's green earth did they not foresee that problem?"

This is where they need to pull more from the budget, or they ask the homeowners for more money, which they always seem to have. The problem is then fixed, and they move on. All of this culminates with the staging and then the big reveal. Finally, the homeowners can see their house for the first time after months of living in a rental, which confirms my suspicions that most Americans are selling meth on the side in order to make all that money. The home, fully staged, always looks beautiful. The couple's expectations are always exceeded, and everyone lives happily ever after. The end.

It's all very nice. It's all very neat. It's all very scripted and it's all very sanitized. And for the audience, it takes about 45 minutes. Well, if you remove the setup and the reveal, the renovation itself actually only takes about 20 minutes. Every renovation we see on TV is just numbers on a screen and a time lapse. Even though we know that everything that went into the renovation was more thoroughly planned, took way more time, and required more sacrifice than what we see, we still want to believe it. We still want to believe that things will be hard but not that hard, costly but not that costly, that problems will arise but that we'll have the resources to fix them, and that the fixing should only take about five minutes of screen time.

In short, we want to believe that the reality of things will be as nice and sanitized as our expectations. I read a quote by J. Gresham Machen the other day that I think is not only insightful here, but everywhere. He said, "Nothing kills true prayer like a shallow optimism." A shallow optimism, or unrealistic expectations destroys projects, relationships, and renovations and even our walk with Christ. In part, this is why I think so many people start projects they never finish.

My wife and I have lived in every house during renovations with our five children and multiple pets. We've learned to embrace the crazy over the years, in part, because we've had to. Renovating and doing the work ourselves was all we could ever afford and living someplace else while the renos were going on simply wasn't an option. In part, because we had no money and, in part, because there really aren't many places for a family of seven with lots of pets to stay for extended periods of time, or any period of time for that matter. Which means we've lived through a lot of crazy. Things always take longer than you think and are more expensive than you think. Very rarely do things go as planned, all the while your tolerance for pain is not nearly as high as you think.

A lot of people give up and quit, or just get terribly discouraged and overwhelmed because things just don't go the way they thought they would. Their expectations are different from reality. Planning to be discouraged and overwhelmed at some point is much different than experiencing that firsthand when you're already exhausted.

None of this means that you don't have expectations and that you don't lay out good plans and count the cost. All of this can reduce any frustration and discouragement. However, we don't live in a world filled with rainbows and puppy dogs, and if things can go wrong they usually do. This isn't bad. This is the school of life. It's this hardship that forces growth, creativity and perseverance. Enduring hardship within a project or a renovation or even a relationship, not only grows you as person through the development that can only be built through hardship, but it also makes the reward that much sweeter in the end.

Dietrich Bonhoeffer, the famed German martyr, who died in a Nazi concentration camp for opposing Hitler said, "When Christ calls a man, He bids him come and die." I think this should be written on the front door of every church. "Churchianity," which is a result of our weak and self-centered worship, has become much like the home shows we watch on TV. Everything is manufactured, marketed, manipulated and sanitized, with a bite-sized sliver of reality mixed in. We live in the real world so we know that things can be hard, but we don't want them to be too hard. We know that following Christ is going to cost us something, but we don't want it to cost us too much. We know we're not perfect, but deep down we think we're actually pretty awesome and that all we need from Christ is a pep talk and a tune up here and there.

Within the church this creates all kinds of false expectations regarding our own walk and life with Christ. The reality is, walking with Christ is far harder than what you initially thought it would be. This is because the condition of your soul is far worse than you thought, and because Christ requires far more of you than you thought. This is why Johnny Cash said, "Being a Christian isn't for sissies. It takes a real man to live for God – a lot more man than to live for the devil."

The reality of the situation is that you are far worse off than you thought, but this is good news because Christ is far better than you can imagine. He who began a good work in you is committed to bringing it through to completion. Are there going to be setbacks along the way? Absolutely, but none of this will stop you from staying on the way. Only when we come to terms with this reality can we begin to actually make progress.

So many worship services today are the equivalent of throwing a fresh coat of paint on rotten walls every week. If sin is mentioned at all, it's usually in a very general and cursory way. We allow for some drama to be interjected here and there as to give the appearance of reality, but in the end everything is resolved. Everybody leaves living happily ever after, at least until next week, and all of this while coming in under 60 minutes from start to finish. It all feels good, like a little evangelical dopamine hit, but in the end that's all it amounts to. It's bound to leave one ultimately overwhelmed and frustrated or delusional when hardship and setbacks come, which they most certainly will.

In Christ, your life is one great big fat renovation project, and He is transforming you into one degree of glory to another. This is often harder than we think it will be and usually requires far more sacrifice than we think it should. However, the reward is far greater than we can imagine, not just in the next life but even now as we strive toward that end.

# Chapter Fifteen

# Cost

W̶e have an expression in our culture, "pay the piper." I can't tell you how many times I have used this expression. It means something like "facing the consequences of your actions." You've done this, that, or the other or have not done this, that or the other, therefore, you are going to have to pay the piper. Just recently, I thought, "I have used this expression several times, and its actually kind of weird. How did this, 'paying the piper,' become associated with facing the consequences of your actions?"

Like any great scholar and theologian, I looked it up online. Some say the story took place as early as the 1200's but the expression was first used in the late 1600's. Here is the story. A town was apparently infested with rats, so they hired a piper who promised to get the rats out of their town. He played his flute luring all of the rats into a nearby river, thus solving the town's problem. When he returned to collect his payment, the townspeople refused to pay him given that the rats were gone. As retribution the piper played his flute luring all of the town's children away. No one knows what happened to the children.

The story is really messed up, but the point holds true. Either way, you are going to have to pay the piper. There is a cost associated with doing business, and we all have to live with the consequences of our actions. We can do what's right and pay that bill on the front end, or we can try to weasel our way out of it, but either way that bill is coming due, and if we have to pay it on the back end, it's going to be much worse.

I suppose there are multiple applications here, but the one I want us to consider is that of cost. Jordon Petersen said, "You are going to pay a price for every bloody thing you do and everything you don't do, you don't get to choose a price. You get to choose which poison you're going to take. That's it." For the townspeople, they were going to pay a price. Either they were going to pay the price of living with the rats or pay someone to remove them. They determined that paying the piper was worth the cost of having the rats removed. Their folly and shame was in thinking they could circumvent responsibility and avoid eating the cost, but life doesn't work that way. Even if it appears possible at times to avoid responsibility, eventually everyone is going to stand before the Almighty, and that is not a tab you want coming due outside of Jesus.

There is a cost associated with everything we do or don't do and there are consequences all the way around and we all get to feast at the table of our own consequences. So then, what's the application regarding home renovation? Well, surprisingly it has nothing to do with rats and more to do with opportunity cost. However, any woman will tell you the cost of removing the rats is worth it, and if finding a literal piper is what you must do than so be it.

It should come as no surprise to anyone that purchasing a home comes at a significant cost. For most people, purchasing a home is the most substantial investment they will ever make. The financial cost of the home is obvious; however, I am specifically thinking here of the incalculable costs of life. The cost of living here as opposed to there. The cost of purchasing this home as opposed to that home.

The cost of buying something new as opposed to the cost of buying something used, and so on.

Life is one great big fat risk, and everything we do has a price tag attached to it. As Petersen said, you are going to pay a price for everything you do or don't do. I don't know who said it, but the saying stuck with me, "If you think trying is hard, wait until you get the bill for not trying." There is a cost for doing something and a cost for not doing something. Risk and the cost-of-living life is like an old saloon door that swings both ways and we should count those costs.

The incalculable cost of life is something that very few people actually think through, at least on any significant level regarding their home. Most people just want to get the nicest house they can, in an area they want to be in and that's that. At a basic foundational level that is certainly true for all of us, and one can hardly be faulted for wanting to get the best bang for their buck.

However, when it comes to our homes and how we want our households to function, I have noticed that people can get paralyzed thinking about all of it. The idea of moving becomes paralyzing, and the idea of renovating seems paralyzing. The idea of paying someone to do the work is scary because there are a lot of snakes out there. The idea of doing any of the work yourself is also scary because of the massive learning curve, which is also not cost free and requires an investiture of time. All of this can lead people into a state of analysis paralysis, and most are then content to stay there because doing nothing seems safer and less costly. But fear is always much more crippling than the financial cost.

Part of the problem is, we think that risk and safety are stagnant things. That is, to stay put and do nothing is safe, and to change is risky. But, as we've seen, there is a cost associated with tolerating a town full of rats. Living with the rats can be much riskier in the long term. Not moving, not renovating, not changing can be more costly in the long run, not just financially, but also in all of the missed opportunities.

Some primary questions that should help us in this regard are, does this home function the way that we need it to? Does this home best facilitate what the Lord has called this family to do? If the answer is yes, then praise God. Outside of the simple upkeep, repairs and maintenance that come with any home you should be good for now. However, as your life changes your home should change along with that, so that your family can always fire on all cylinders.

Answering these questions also puts any type of renovation into perspective. As your life changes, your home should change along with it. Your primary concern being function. How can your family best operate in the space that you are currently living in? The primary concern is the function of your household, the flourishing of your family, and your calling/s before God. You can make anything pretty, once those questions are answered.

In answering those questions, it gives you something to shoot for. Itemize everything on your list. Perhaps you need a space for homeschooling, or perhaps your kitchen cannot accommodate all of your fellowship needs, or even just your large family. Maybe the home you purchased when it was just the two of you was awesome…for just the two of you, but now your family has grown, and something has to change to make it function better.

I thought our first home was awesome. It felt like a castle when it was just the two of us, but not so much five kids later. With a small kitchen, only one full bath and a busy road out front it no longer functioned well for us. We could have potentially made more renovations or additions to accommodate our growing family, but it would have been a poor investment for that home, and it wouldn't have fixed the busy road, so we moved. Was it scary? Yes, at the time. Were costs involved? Certainly. But the cost of staying was riskier than moving.

These are questions that we have asked ourselves, and had to answer several times over now, regarding our church and our family and everything related therein. There is always a cost of doing business and there is always a cost of not doing business, and we all have to figure out what that is for our families. Jesus said this,

> Whoever does not bear his own cross and come after me cannot be my disciple. For which of you, desiring to build a tower, does not first sit down and count the cost, whether he has enough to complete it? Otherwise, when he has laid a foundation and is not able to finish, all who see it begin to mock him, saying, 'This man began to build and was not able to finish.' Or what king, going out to encounter another king in war, will not sit down first and deliberate whether he is able with ten thousand to meet him who comes against him with twenty thousand? And if not, while the other is yet a great way off, he sends a delegation and asks for terms of peace. So therefore, any one of you who does not renounce all that he has cannot be my disciple. (Luke 14:27-33)

Your life is a gift, and your home is a gift, you might as well make them both awesome, so that you can live a life well-pleasing to the Lord. Best to use those talents instead of burying them.

# Chapter Sixteen

# Time

Time is a funny thing, or at least our relationship with it is a funny thing. Out of all the resources we have at our disposal in life including time, talents and treasure, time is the one resource we can never get back and yet it's the one that we tend to think we have an endless amount of. I believe it was William Penn who said, "Time is what we want most, but what we use worst."

Treasures can be gained and lost, squandered and hoarded. Talents can be gained and lost, refined and neglected. But time, that's a one and done. Every single second, every single moment of your life is like watching the waves continually ripple in. There is no pause or rewind button (or back arrow if you're a certain age) in life. It just doesn't work that way.

I remember back when my wife was pregnant with our first. It seems like it was a lifetime ago. Probably, because it was. So many people told us to appreciate the time because it goes so fast. I would smile and agree as if I knew what they were talking about, and honestly, at the time, I thought I did. In actuality, I didn't have a clue. But now that I am gray, and our firstborn is eighteen I remember what all the gray heads told me then and I look back and wish I was able to understand those same words the way I do now.

As a country, we are divided on just about everything, or so it seems. However, I reckon that the one thing we can all agree on is that time goes by too fast. One minute you are holding your babies and strapping them into car seats, and the next minute they are driving.

Unfortunately, you need to get a few years on you before you understand the brevity of life. When you understand this, it should help you to prioritize your life. As leadership guru John C. Maxwell says, "Time management is an oxymoron. Time is beyond our control, and the clock keeps ticking regardless of how we lead our lives. Priority management is the answer to maximizing the time we have."

All of this is important regarding our homes. Time goes by so fast, which means there is more than just a financial cost to any project we may or may not take on. The cost of moving, the cost of renovating, the size and scope of the renovation, or whether to take on either, all have a cost that is not just financial. We have to try to balance all of these costs, what we can quantify and what we can't with what we believe the Lord has for our lives, and the vision that we have for our families. What is going to be sacrificed and what is going to be gained? You don't get to choose whether or not you are going to pay a price, but you do get to choose what price to pay.

These are important questions to ask and answer, in part because they put you in the position of living your life instead of your life living you. You begin with principles and priorities, that is, the things that are most important to you and the vision that you have for your life and your household. After that, you seek to conform your surroundings to that with the goal that it will help your household flourish. Regarding your home, you want to act and not react. You want to be driven by purpose and not by conformity to a cultural standard. You don't want to be driven by materialism, or vanity, or competition, life is too short for that nonsense.

However, because life changes so quickly so too do the needs of your home, and you want your home to accommodate those needs. The smoother the flow and function of your home the more productive your family will be, which can reduce frustration and increase joy. That is not to say that environment is the sole contributor to either frustration or joy, but it certainly is a contributor. When you have a certain vision for your home and it doesn't function well, that will create tension.

This is why it's important for a husband and wife to sit down and put together their wish lists, based on what they envision for their home and based on their priorities. Do you work from home? What kind of work do you do? Do you homeschool? What is most important to you – square footage or acreage? If you can get both that would be awesome, but usually there is a trade-off. Do you want to be in close proximity to your family, friends, school, church, and work? Are you dead set on a particular area or neighborhood? That will determine a lot. If you can't afford all you want, are you willing to take on a renovation? Again, you don't get to choose whether or not to pay a price, but you do get to choose what price you pay.

The way you answer these questions will determine a lot. For example, if you are dead set on a particular area, but can only afford a two-bedroom home in that area and you have a family of six, then it's going to be really hard for your family to flourish there and you need to reevaluate things. We can't have it all, but we can have what we are willing to prioritize. When we think we can have it all we usually burn ourselves out chasing after the wind by acquiring things that should be much lower on the priority list.

You begin with the vision, the foundation of which should be a godly marriage that makes lots of godly babies that grow up in a godly home filled with a bunch of godly joy and laughter and feasting. Is your home a place where you all can flourish and grow? If not, why not? I bet the way you answered that question has little to do with your actual brick and mortar home and more to do with the quality of the relationships that fill your home. This is fitting because this is what you are seeking to build. Everything else environmentally should then be shaped around that.

Also, when those priorities and principles are determined, they help you to know what to take on and when, if at all. It's like that great theologian Kenny Rogers said, "You got to know when to hold 'em, know when to fold 'em, know when to walk away, and know when to run." Your priorities for your home should shape the use of your time and allow your home to flourish. The things that bring flourishing, you keep, and the things that don't, you throw away.

Men, we can't expect our wives and children to flourish in our homes if we're not willing to set them up for success. Considering available time, talents and treasure, a husband and wife should sit down and figure out what's most important to them and then get busy making that happen. Most people think that just wishing it so is enough – it's not! You have to have those conversations and you have to get after it today because tomorrow is coming.

Most people don't live their lives, their lives live them. Time is going to keep moving whether you like it or not. You don't want to look back with regret, "coulda-shoulda-woulda" is not a pleasant, or fruitful way to live.

> Lord, you have been our dwelling place in all generations. Before the mountains were brought forth, or ever you had formed the earth and the world, from everlasting to everlasting you are God. You return man to dust and say, "Return, O children of man!" For a thousand years in your sight are but as yesterday when it is past, or as a watch in the night. You sweep them away as with a flood; they are like a dream, like grass that is renewed in the morning: in the morning it flourishes and is renewed; in the evening it fades and withers. For we are brought to an end by your anger; by your wrath we are dismayed. You have set our iniquities before you, our secret sins in the light of your presence. For

all our days pass away under your wrath; we bring our years to an end like a sigh. The years of our life are seventy, or even by reason of strength eighty; yet their span is but toil and trouble; they are soon gone, and we fly away. Who considers the power of your anger, and your wrath according to the fear of you? So teach us to number our days that we may get a heart of wisdom. (Psalm 90:1-12)

## Chapter Seventeen

# Write Your Plans in Pencil

The best way to work is to plan your work and work your plan. As a general principle this much is true, it's best to plan your work. However, it is also true that when writing out our plans, it is best to always write them in pencil. Heraclitus said we never step in the same river twice. His point being that the only constant in life is that everything changes. As a starting point for all of life, as a Christian, we would certainly disagree with that statement taken *en toto*. Some things are absolute, certain, immovable, and indubitable. However, as a general observation regarding life, change is kind of hard to deny.

The reason I bring this up is because even if we have the best laid plans imaginable, there are still a great multitude of variables outside of our control. Sure, we try to plan for all of them, and we should, however, the unexpected is, well, unexpected. Can you factor in a margin for the unexpected? Yes, but not with any degree of specificity or accuracy. Therefore, operationally in all of life, but certainly regarding any degree of home renovation you will have to be adaptable.

It's like that great theologian Mike Tyson said, "Everyone has a plan until they get punched in the mouth." The home we are currently renovating has punched us in the face and punched us in the face a lot. If everything that we wanted to do had been written in stone, then it would have crushed us. This is where it is always helpful to continually ask what your desires are for your home. If you know the vision that you have for your home, it will enable you to prioritize your budget and projects and keep you focused when a punch comes your way.

Before we purchased our current home, we bought it sight unseen out of state. We just assumed there would be certain things that a realtor would catch and make known to us, not so much. We also assumed that there would be certain things that an inspector would catch and make known to us, not so much. Let's just say that where we moved to, from where we moved from is a little more laid back. That easygoing mentality is magnificent in some respects, not so much in others, and unfortunately for us this cultural intelligence was acquired only through boots on the ground. Because of this, what we anticipated to spend on the renovation was way off. Needless to say, that changed our plans quite a bit.

Before we took occupancy, we had a lot of fun anticipating all of the things we were going to do to the home and how we were going to do it. We also made our best guestimates as to how long it would take and how much it would cost. Looking back on those conversations we laugh, and maybe cry a little too. We thought we would have enough in the budget to get a pool, which the kids would love and would be worthwhile since we were moving to a much warmer environment, and it could be used the vast majority of the year.

This was destroyed when we realized, basically in our first walk through, that we had foundation issues, which to correct, turned out to be just as much as a pool. Well, that was a big fat punch in the mouth. As bad as that was, none of that changed what we envisioned for our home. All this little setback did was force us to become more strategic with our time. We now take repeated trips to the coast as a family, which has turned out to be a tremendous blessing for us. Life punches you in the face, so you adapt. What we desired for our family hadn't changed. We just needed to change our strategy to get from A to B, which we did.

So much of life is knowing when to push and when to pull. You need a plan. However, any plan is always meant to serve the broader vision. The strategy always changes based on new information and variables, which you have to be willing to adapt to if you want to reach the same vision. Our broader vision is what we desire for our marriage, our family, and our work. Any type of renovation that we do or take on is always subservient to that.

The whole foundation debacle, which was just one of many debacles, also had a ripple effect elsewhere. The home we purchased has a basement, which is kind of like a unicorn where we are located. We thought this was great, not just for novelties sake, but because we thought we could use this additional space for storage and a podcast studio. Well, the new beams and framing that were required for the foundation changed the basement layout quite a bit.

As it turns out the new layout actually worked better for us than we were envisioning. The studio ended up being smaller than what we envisioned, but that's fine. Again, the goal was to have a studio, which we were able to accomplish. Who cares if it didn't happen exactly as we originally planned. The route changed, but the destination didn't. Mission accomplished. The hardest thing to deal with at the time were the delays. We anticipated that we wouldn't be able to record any new material for one month. It turned out to be five. However, by God's grace, this enabled me to write more. Praise God.

Proverbs 21:31 says, "The horse is made ready for the day of battle, but the victory belongs to the LORD." We work, we strategize, we make plans, but things change, and things come up all of the time. Some of those things are big and some of those things are small, some of those things require a big pivot and some a small pivot. It is important to note that the plan is never the end. It is only meant to direct you to the end. When setbacks, challenges, or distractions come, which they will, then you adapt. The mission hasn't changed, but the route has. At that point, you make the necessary adjustments and enjoy the scenery change.

Paul was the greatest missionary of all time and he constantly had to deal with setbacks, face punches and audibles called directly by the Holy Spirit.

> And they went through the region of Phrygia and Galatia, having been forbidden by the Holy Spirit to speak the word in Asia. And when they had come up to Mysia, they attempted to go into Bithynia, but the Spirit of Jesus did not allow them. So, passing by Mysia, they went down to Troas. And a vision appeared to Paul in the night: a man of Macedonia was standing there, urging him and saying, "Come over to Macedonia and help us." And when Paul had seen the vision, immediately we sought to go on into Macedonia, concluding that God had called us to preach the gospel to them. (Acts 16:6-10)

Was Paul's desire to bring the Gospel to Mysia and Bithynia a good desire? Absolutely, it was, in fact he was called by God, specifically to bring the Gospel to the Gentiles. However, it was either not the right timing, or he was not the right person, or perhaps there was some other reason. Either way, Paul was forbidden by the Holy Spirit from going there. Paul's plans changed but his mission didn't. From Paul's perspective the Spirit called an audible. Paul said yes and amen, and his time in Macedonia was blessed.

In all of this, I am not minimizing the importance of having a plan. Jesus Himself illustrates the importance of careful planning. "For which of you, desiring to build a tower, does not first sit down and count the cost, whether he has enough to complete it? Otherwise, when he has laid a foundation and is not able to finish, all who see it begin to mock him, saying, 'This man began to build and was not able to finish.'" (Luke 14:28-30).

Not only is it important to plan, but even more important and perhaps a prolegomena to that, is seeking the Lord's will before considering any type of plan. "Unless the LORD builds the house, those who build it labor in vain. Unless the LORD watches over the city, the watchman stays awake in vain." (Psalm 127:1).

Even the best laid plans need to be adaptable, in every area of your life. However, just because the plans change doesn't mean the mission or the vision changes. On the contrary, as things change and new information is acquired, the plan changes to accomplish the mission, which was the purpose of making the plan in the first place. Make plans, yes, but make sure you write them down in pencil.

# Chapter Eighteen

# Kill Your Ego and Get Your Hands Dirty

In the year 2000, lightning struck with arguably the greatest cinematic masterpiece of all time. That was the year that Ridley Scott's *Gladiator* was released in theaters. *Gladiator* stars Russell Crowe as Roman General Maximus Decimus Meridius, who was a loyal servant to Emperor Marcus Aurelius. Marcus was murdered by his whiny little entitled son, Commodus, who then tries to kill Maximus, but because Maximus is so awesome he escapes death. However, before Maximus can travel all the way home to protect his wife and son, Commodus has them killed.

An injured Maximus is then discovered and taken by slave traders where he is then forced to fight in the arena. Because Maximus is super awesome, he kills everyone in the arena that they put in there with him, which earns him a spot to fight in Rome. It is here Maximus comes face to face with Emperor Commodus, the man who tried to have him killed and who killed his family. There is some back and forth between them, but what is really awesome is what Maximus says to Commodus, "My name is Maximus Decimus Meridius, Commander of the Armies of the North, General of the Felix Legions, loyal servant to the true emperor, Marcus Aurelius. Father to a murdered son, husband to a murdered wife. And I will have my vengeance, in this life or the next." BOOM!

Fast forward a bit and Maximus gets his vengeance by killing Commodus in the arena, but Maximus dies as well. The end. The reason I bring this up is because every time Maximus prepares for battle or before he lays the Stone Cold Smackdown in the arena we always see him kneeling down and picking up some dirt that he then runs through his hands. Why exactly does he do this? Not sure, but it looks pretty awesome. Maybe it helps his grip on his sword, maybe he is reminding himself of his own mortality – from dust you are and to dust you will return, maybe he just does it because it looks cool, or maybe he is just saying literally and metaphorically, "I am about to get my hands dirty." Again, BOOM!

Ok, back to why I brought this up in the first place. It's because it was the coolest way I could think of to illustrate to you that if you are going to embark on any type of renovation, you are going to have to humble yourself and get your hands dirty. BOOM!

Pretty much every single home show, or at least it feels like it, has a woman lead who is a designer. She is usually portrayed as the ultimate boss bitch who has total control over everything. Her husband is either there for some comic relief to make sure that his boss bitch wife is still likeable and relatable (while still being better than you), or to at least make sure momma gets what momma wants.

At the beginning of the show, she meets with her clients who are usually portrayed as dupes that she is there to save, which she summarily does within the twenty-five-minute mark. Nevertheless, before the big reveal we have to see her in action, and when I say in action I don't mean Wendy from Bob the Builder action. Oh no! This boss bitch comes to the work site in high heels and tight pants, with freshly manicured nails and occasionally with her boobs hanging out. It is here that she is fully equipped for her photo op, usually with a brand new toolbelt on.

I know this is not true across the board, and many of these women have worked hard to get to where they are and have rightly earned the success they have. However, the stereotype and trope hold true, nonetheless. Much of this has to do with producers that need these women portrayed in this way because the audience eats it up. Regardless, these reality shows are anything but reality.

These shows are entertaining, and the work that is actually done on the homes is real, however, these shows are as manicured and manufactured as most of their stars. If you watch these shows and expect your experience to be just as manicured, then you will be disappointed. Ladies, you're not going to get that project done in high heels or without messing up that nice manicure. Guys, you are not getting any projects done without getting your clothes dirty and needing pain meds later.

Prepare to be humbled. You're not a construction god or a designer goddess. You're going to get messy. You're going to get dirty. You're going to be tired and uncomfortable. You're going to deal with people that are going to do shoddy work and try to screw you over. You're often going to have to call audibles and manipulate your budget to the best of your ability. You're going to repeatedly take two steps forward and one step back, and multiple times over you're going to feel like you hit your limit.

All of this happens on these shows as well, you just don't see the full extent of it and if you do, you never feel the full effect. It is always edited to make everyone on the show appear like they know what they are doing all the time with minimal mess and discomfort. What mess or trouble they do show usually only lasts about five minutes of screen time before a resolution is reached or the mess is cleaned up.

The cold hard truth is that if you are going into any project or into any situation in life with the boss bitch attitude, thinking you know everything and have it all together, you are going to be forced to eat a piece of humble pie. And this is God's mercy upon your life because it will humble you and force you to learn.

Pride kills in life and kills in renovations, and when you're dealing with other people's homes or your own, that's not cool. Pride is also the reason why so many married couples won't work on renovations together, or when they do, they are at each other's throats.

Working on projects with my wife is the most rewarding thing for me. We equally take joy and pride in our home knowing that we get to work on it together and as a family. If my wife took a boss bitch attitude, I would shut down and go build a nice little enclosure on the corner of our roof top. If I was a domineering know-it-all jerk, my wife would shut down and would never want to help, nor should she. Needless to say, if that was the case we would never put our hands to the plow and reach our goals together.

As in renovations, so too in life, if you approach them with a spirit of humility, desirous to learn and eager to help, you'll probably learn and grow in many ways and rejoice much when the projects are over. The Scriptures have much to say about humility. Here are just a few verses to help us on our way.

> The fear of the LORD is instruction in wisdom, and humility comes before honor. (Proverbs 15:33)

> Therefore it says, "God opposes the proud but gives grace to the humble." Submit yourselves therefore to God. Resist the devil, and he will flee from you. Draw near to God, and he will draw near to you. Cleanse your hands, you sinners, and purify your hearts, you double-minded. Be wretched and mourn and weep. Let your laughter be turned to mourning and your joy to gloom. Humble yourselves before the Lord, and he will exalt you. (James 4:6-10)

Humble yourselves, therefore, under the mighty hand of God so that at the proper time he may exalt you, casting all your anxieties on him, because he cares for you. (1 Peter 5:6)

This is the uniform witness throughout the Scriptures. If you are proud, you are going to be brought low. If you have a spirit of humility, God will exalt you at the proper time. So then, kill your ego, and dive into everything that the Lord puts in front of you. Be willing to learn and then get your hands dirty, and then do it again. Maybe even go find a little dirt to run through your hands. BOOM!

## Chapter Nineteen

# A Little Bit Each Day

"Just a little bit each day," is a saying we use all the time in our house. Living in a constant state of renovation, with projects endlessly staring you in the face, seemingly not just saying to me, "finish me," but "finish me now," can be overwhelming. There is a fine line between chaos and dominion, and unfortunately, more often than not it feels like I am crotching that tight rope.

With that being said, you can lose your mind if you're not careful. If you take any one thing, one task, or one project in isolation it's usually not enough to break you and make you want to curl up in the fetal position and weep like a little girl. But taken together, the magnitude of the work seems impossible to complete and can lead you into a state of analysis paralysis. Or even worse, you can feel like good Pilgrim locked up in Giant Despair's castle.

It is true, you have to keep your eyes on the big picture, but that's not what you are going to accomplish on any given day. If that were the case, your vision would be far too small in any area of your life. So, what do you do? You do a little bit each day. You can't do everything, but you can still do something, so every day you have to do a little of the something that you can do.

There are days where I just put up one piece of trim or move materials from the garage to the house in preparation for the next project, just to say I did something. Will a project ever get done moving at that pace? Probably not, but that's not the point. The point is that you keep moving forward. Even if it's very slow at times, you're always moving in the same direction.

That great theologian Rocky Balboa said to Creed about winning a fight, you take it "One step at a time. One punch at a time. One round at a time." Every home we've bought has needed more work than the last because apparently our memories of labor, sweat and tears have been forgotten. Far too often we are like a happy mother of a toddler that looks back and thinks, "Labor wasn't really that bad."

Therefore, at some point in the renovation, we always have what we will just call a "moment." You know, one of those moments that forces you to question all of your life decisions. You look around overwhelmed and think, "This is impossible." And honestly, in that moment, it is. Because you're trying to do everything all at once. You're trying to build Rome in a day and that's not happening.

However, if you keep moving forward, steadily plodding through what's in front of you, eventually you will accomplish much and the impossible seems to have a funny way of being forgotten. Steady plodding is a principle that can be applied to anything in your life. Solomon says it this way regarding wealth generation, "Wealth gained hastily will dwindle, but whoever gathers little by little will increase it." (Prov. 13:11). The story of "The Tortoise and the Hare" is familiar to most of us, and its wisdom is easily understood, but very rarely applied.

This happened with all of my kids. That is, they got to a point where their reading level catapulted them into bigger books. At some point, they said, "I can't read that, it's too big." Then I would ask them, "How do we read a book?" They would usually just stare at me. Then I would answer, "One page at a time." I would tell them I don't want them to sit and read the entire book today. I just want you to read one page. Pretty soon the book was done, and they were on to the next impossible task.

Another way we say this is, "How do you eat a whale?" Answer, "One bite at a time." Yes, we need to have big dreams and big visions. Yes, we need to pray big and get after it. There is certainly nothing wrong with wanting to accomplish much. But on a daily basis what you need to do is just a little bit each day…keep moving forward, and never stop moving forward. Of course, some days will be more productive than others, but sometimes those days where you are just able to do a little bit are tremendous victories because you kept the ball moving forward.

This is also a wonderful principle in relation to your walk with Christ. So many of us can get discouraged at how much unlike Jesus we are or how little progress we seem to be making. Yes, Christ likeness is the goal, but I got news for you – you're not going to accomplish that today! The best that we can hope for is to be faithful with the time that we've been given and the time that we've been given is today. If you focus on daily faithfulness, or the slow, upward climb in the same direction you'll end up with a faithful life.

Yes, we need to think big, but often that is accomplished by small actions over and over again until you reach your goal or get to your destination. A little bit each day is all it takes.

# Chapter Twenty

# Eyes on the Prize

I was born in the late 70's which means I grew up basking in the glow of all of the 80's goodness. I love action movies and just about every 80's action hero was over the top. All muscled up and unstoppable, think Rambo and Commando and the like. I saved up twenty bucks from a couple of birthdays, and I bought my first barbell set from Montgomery Wards. It was a little twenty-pound set with four five-pound sanded weights, with a blue hollow bar that was three feet long. I still remember it. I would do every exercise I could, but mostly just curls for hours.

Needless to say, when I was a kid nobody had to tell me to workout. I loved working out. The coolest thing in the world was when a friend would let me use one of their guest passes at the gym to workout with them. I had no money for a gym membership, or even for a day pass, so when I could go I would pack a lunch and stay there all day. The gym was this amazing world filled with possibility and promise. Being there made me feel awesome and rich, if only for a few hours.

I say all this because you didn't have to force me to be there. Nobody had to convince me that I needed to go to the gym. The harder the workout the better. The more I learned the better. I think people learn to love the process if they love the prize that the process produces. People can endure just about anything if they can see the end of what that anything will produce.

I think there are very important principles here for us to keep in mind for all of life. Paul said this to Timothy,

> You then, my child, be strengthened by the grace that is in Christ Jesus, and what you have heard from me in the presence of many witnesses entrust to faithful men, who will be able to teach others also. Share in suffering as a good soldier of Christ Jesus. No soldier gets entangled in civilian pursuits, since his aim is to please the one who enlisted him. An athlete is not crowned unless he competes according to the rules. It is the hard-working farmer who ought to have the first share of the crops. Think over what I say, for the Lord will give you understanding in everything. (2 Tim. 2:1-7)

What in the world does a soldier, an athlete, and a farmer have in common? We see the end for which they all strive. For the soldier, it was to please the one who enlisted him. For the athlete, it was to wear the crown. For the farmer, it was to share in the crops. In fact, when we think of any of these vocations this is generally where our minds go, that is, to the end product.

However, the vast majority of the soldier's time is not spent in battle. His time is spent training and preparing, without which he would be easily defeated in battle bringing no pleasure to the one who enlisted him. It's the same way with the athlete. The majority of his time is spent in training and in the grind. Very little of his time is actually spent in the games that lead to his reward, but all of his time invested in training is for that end. It's true of the farmer as well. Early mornings and late nights, constantly grinding so that he can reap the harvest. Without all that labor there would be no harvest.

With all of these vocations, it's the grind that matters. The cumulative effect of it is what produces the reward. Day after day, night after night, week after week, month after month with seemingly no reward, and then the battle is won, the games are won, and the harvest is reaped. It is the end that enables you to grind through all the hardship, all the mundane, all the seemingly lack of progress. When you are grinding and laboring without end, you have to be able to see the end to keep going. When that is the case, the grind can actually become enjoyable.

This is going to sound overly dramatic, and perhaps it is, first world problems after all, but the point remains. Often times when working on a renovation, especially if you are doing the work yourself and living in the home during it, it can feel like a grind. Early on, the work seems to be endless, and you seem to be getting nowhere. You are working on the really important stuff that nobody will ever see, and that's usually after weeks of demo. Before getting to the really rewarding stuff, which is the whole reason why you decided to do a renovation in the first place, you have the grind.

When you can't see the end or the reward in front of you, you have to see it in your mind. You have to remind yourself why you started all this work in the first place. You have to see how your life will function better, and how enjoyable that will be. You have to remind yourself that even though there seems to be no reward day after day, there is movement, there is progress and to keep plowing away. You have to remind yourself that all of the inconvenience and discomfort will be eclipsed by the glory of receiving your reward.

In Hebrews 11, not only are we told that faith enables you to see the unseeable, but we are given several examples of this faith exercised in the life of God's people. We are able to see the endurance and perseverance that were produced by such faith. They were able to endure, sometimes horrific things because they could see the reward of their faith, though they currently didn't possess what was promised. They believed the promise of that reward and were able to see it, at least in part, by faith.

We then read in the beginning of Hebrews 12,

> Therefore, since we are surrounded by so great a cloud of witnesses, let us also lay aside every weight, and sin which clings so closely, and let us run with endurance the race that is set before us, looking to Jesus, the founder and perfector of our faith, who for the joy that was set before him endured the cross, despising the shame, and is seated at the right hand of the throne of God. (Heb.12:1-2)

Jesus is the founder and perfector of our faith, and He is the ultimate, perfect example of keeping His eyes on the prize. The joy that was set before Him, wasn't the cross *per se*. He endured the cross because of the joy that was set before Him. The joy that was set before Him was the vindication of His Father's holiness, and the outpouring of His Father's mercy, both of which were on magnificent display on the cross. The joy that was set before Him was His exaltation to the Father's right hand, as the perfect, obedient God-man.

So much of the Christian life is just grinding it out. Pursuing faithfulness day after day, week after week, month after month, and often from our perspective, with seemingly little progress. But the grind is where all the progress is made. It is the grind that prepares you for the battle, for the games, and for the harvest, which is exactly what you have to set your sights on as you grind.

As in home renovations so too in life, the reward always comes later. It comes after all the sweat and labor, after the grind, but it does come. Which is why you have to keep grinding to that end remembering why you began in the first place.

# Chapter Twenty One

# Cry It Out and Then Move On

Our first house was built in 1932 and had all of the charm of an old home. For anyone who has ever owned an old home you know that the word "charm" is code for a home filled with a lot of awesome features that you do not get in homes today where nothing is level and there are lots of issues. We loved that home and had all of our babies there, so we have lots of fond memories of our time there and always felt blessed to have that home. However, coupled with those fond memories, are memories that are not as fond.

I remember I had just redone our dining room ceiling. Originally, it had beautiful thick crown molding but there were some plaster issues that needed to be re-done. The easiest way for me to fix the plaster at the time was to remove the crown, which did not want to be removed. In fact, it had a symbiotic relationship with the ceiling. Which is a way of saying that they were in covenant union and had become one flesh. Which is a pleasant way of saying I jacked up my beautiful old crown molding getting it off. And by jacked it up, I mean I pretty much destroyed it.

However, I was determined to make lemonade out of lemons. I ended up installing a squared board and batten over the whole ceiling and then squared off the crown to match my board and batten molding. It looked pretty grand and fit with the aesthetics of an old home. I have always loved doing ceilings, which nobody was really doing at the time, so I thought I was pretty awesome. I think we were all in on this project about five hundred bucks which was a fortune for us at the time, but we fixed the problem, and it was a good investment in awesomeness.

Refinishing the dining room was important to us because that's where our children did their schooling, and we had just bought a new table determined to have meals together. This was important to us because we grew up in front of the TV, eating TV dinners at a tray table. That to say, we thought the investment was worth it given the priority this room had in our lives.

About a week after I finished, which was still soon enough for me to be radiating my awesome glow, my wife and I were sitting in the living room. The living room and dining room were right next to each other so you could see the majority of each room from the other. We were in Michigan at the time, and spring was just beginning which meant so too was the rain. As the rain poured down outside, it kind of, maybe just maybe started to sound like it wasn't just raining outside.

I thought to myself, "Self, that is weird, what do you think that constantly dripping sound is that sounds like water coming in the house?" And then myself answered me, "Self, it must be water coming in the house." But then I told myself, "That can't be because it sounds like it's coming from our newly finished dining room." So, then I told myself that I better check it out. Turns out, I didn't even need to get off the couch to begin my investigative journey. I could see the water coming in from the corner of the ceiling. Well, that sucks!

What do you do? Try to dry up the mess and wait for it to stop raining and then begin your investigative journey. When things like this happen, having a pity party for yourself isn't going to help anything. However, things like this truly suck. So sometimes you need to allow yourself a minute to cry it out so that you can move on. Not that I have ever cried, but I have heard that it's helpful for some. Being frustrated is totally normal, but your frustration won't fix the problem. So, give yourself a hot minute, and then get back at it.

The interesting thing is the leaking ceiling/wall was directly next to our flat-roof garage (which is the stupidest thing ever) that we just replaced. After contacting the roofing company, they came out and redid the flashing. Problem solved, right? Nope. As it turns out the wood underneath the metal sill of the door that led out onto the flat roof (again, stupid) had rotted allowing water to get in. Now that we had identified the problem we could fix it, which we did.

I can't tell you how many times we have had setbacks with projects over the years. We were so happy to be done with a project and just when we were feeling good about ourselves, it felt like someone snuck up and punched us in the face. Not cool! Sometimes, before you even have time to recover you get punched again. Super not cool!

My most favorite poem of all time is Rudyard Kipling's, "If." I read it often because it keeps me going and reminds me that it's ok to cry it out (metaphorically speaking), sometimes, but also, that you can't stay there too long. One stanza reads as follows,

> If you can dream – and not make dreams your master; If you can think – and not make thoughts your aim; If you can meet with Triumph and Disaster and treat those two imposters just the same; If you can bear to hear the truth you've spoken twisted by knaves to make a trap for fools, or watch the things you gave your life to, broken, and stoop and build 'em up with worn-out tools.

It is one thing to build something, but then to go back and rebuild it or fix it after it's been destroyed because of no fault of your own, literally with worn out tools, takes grit. It sounds silly because it's just regarding a home project, but home projects are very personal, and you usually have lots invested, not just financially but physically and emotionally.

If you do enough projects or are just beginning to renovate a space in your house or your entire house, you are going to get kicked in the nuts on occasion and it's never pleasant. But you have to step back, acknowledge the reality of the situation, detach yourself from it in order to get perspective. Give yourself a minute, figure out what went wrong, and then get busy fixing it.

This is a principle that applies to every area of your life, especially your walk with the Lord. There have been so many times in my life when something terrible happened and I have just been ready to throw in the towel. You start having a pity party for yourself. You know that these things happen to people, but why you? God must have gotten the names mixed up. Remembering that you are not alone in anything that you go through doesn't take away the pain or the frustration, but it can help to put it in perspective.

I think of some varsity level saints that were just ready to be done and tap out. Elijah comes to mind, so does Jeremiah. Heck, Jeremiah was known as the weeping prophet. Even Jonah told God that he wanted to die, but that was a little different because all his wounds were self-inflicted.

Even Jesus Christ, the Son of God come in the flesh was called the man of sorrows. The author of Hebrews says this, "Therefore he had to be made like his brothers in every respect, so that he might become a merciful and faithful high priest in the service of God, to make propitiation for the sins of the people. For because he himself has suffered when tempted, he is able to help those who are being tempted." (Heb. 2:17-18).

There is absolutely nothing that we are going through or will go through or can go through, that Jesus hasn't already gone through for us. There is nothing that we can go through that He doesn't understand. When we suffer, or struggle or are tempted, He is able to help us. He understands completely and He is a compassionate God.

Regardless of how big the setback or the trial may be, that doesn't change the mission. That doesn't change why you started. That doesn't really change anything. The only thing that actually changes in these scenarios is you, as you seek the Lord in them. And though it doesn't feel like it at the time, that's actually a good thing. Therefore, whether that setback is small or big, rest in Christ who will carry you through it, and don't be afraid to cry it out and move on (hypothetically speaking of course).

# Chapter Twenty Two

# Embrace the Suck

Though no one is quite sure of the origins of the military mantra, "Embrace the Suck," we know it was popularized during the Iraq war. Now, "Embrace the suck" can mean a multitude of things and be applied in a multitude of ways. It can mean taking personal responsibility. It can mean, "figure it out." It can mean persevering through trials. It can mean, "plans change – adapt." It can mean, doing hard things and not whining about it. It can mean, the embrace of hardship. It can mean, never giving up, and so on.

Life can be tough, and hardships are real. You cannot ignore them, and you cannot deny them. In many respects these hardships and challenges need to be "embraced" so that you can move through them. Not that life sucks, but on a most basic level, embracing the suck simply means embracing reality. As Ayn Rand said, "You can deny reality, but you cannot deny it's consequences." When life bites, you kick it back in the teeth.

"Embrace the suck" is really the perfect mantra for life under the sun. There are glimpses of glory in the world, but this world is fallen and everyone reading this knows the world is not all sunshine and puppy dogs. Some things truly do suck. Some of these things are of our own making. Some of these things are of other's makings that we are directly and indirectly influenced by. There is real evil in the world that creates terrible situations and does horrible things. Then there are simply circumstances that have nothing to do with people, they are just unfortunate or create much pain and discomfort.

What does any of this have to do with home renovation? Much and in every way. I say, "embrace the suck," out loud to myself just about every day. In fact, before writing this I began tearing out the baseboards in our master suite. I knew there was water damage underneath one of our windows because I could see it in the subfloor after I ripped out the carpet. Of course, none of this was caught on the inspection because inspections are pretty much useless, unless you are an insurance company or a bank.

After removing the baseboards, I could see that the drywall was basically mush. After pushing my finger through it, I could feel that everything behind it was also mush. I thought to myself, "So not cool!" Why? Because there was supposed to be 2x4's where my finger now was. Well, there was a 2x4 there, or at least the remains of one. As I began tearing out the subfloor, I could see that the point where the two joists meet on our sill plate were both rotten at least a foot and a half back in both directions.

Well, that sucks! As I write this, I don't know just how extensive the damage is yet, and how much time and money it will cost me to fix. Either way, my response is the same. The problem will be fixed, and the obstacle will be overcome. We will crush it and move on. Every obstacle may slow the advance for a time, but it won't stop it. Am I happy about it? Does my answer to that question matter one way or another?

All these obstacles and roadblocks and setbacks that we face in life are simply the weight training of life. In order for your muscles to grow they need constant stress and resistance. We grow as humans in very much the same way. By overcoming challenges and resistance. Are we happy about it when these challenges arise? No, that's why we call them hardships, challenges, trials and so on. The joy isn't in the trial. The joy is in overcoming it, and crushing it, and then moving on to the next. This is where and how we grow.

You can do everything in life to avoid challenges, avoid hardship and to avoid risk of any kind. But as the man in the Parable of the Talents found out, when you bury your talents in the ground as to try to avoid any loss, you end up losing much more. You don't get a choice as to whether or not you are going to face some sucky things in life, but you can choose to either embrace them and crush them or ignore them and be crushed by them.

In every home that we have remodeled, in a great multitude of ways we have faced much suck. At times the suck has felt seemingly endless. With each new suck, I think, this far surpasses the old suck, and this new suck seems to be beyond my ability to deal with and/or cope with. And honestly, it is until it's crushed. Bench pressing 400 pounds is impossible if your max weight is only 100 pounds. In fact, if you tried to lift it you would probably be seriously hurt. That is, until you repeatedly and constantly embrace new and harder resistance every time out. Before you know it, what seemed impossible has been overcome and is now commonplace.

How should Christians approach life? Well, they should embrace the suck. Now, simply saying this is probably enough to give certain respectable types wedgies, so it's important to clarify some things. I am not saying that everything sucks – just deal with it. No, but I am acknowledging the reality of the situation. The Lord could be using the suckiness to discipline, instruct, humble and strengthen His children. There is much good that can come out on the other end of the suckiness.

For the joy that was set before Him, Jesus endured the cross. The cross sucked, in fact, we can rightly say that it was the suckiest thing to ever happen in human history. Yet, Jesus endured it with joy because of what it accomplished. Again, this is to acknowledge the reality of the situation without denying the actual suckiness of the situation. We glory in the cross not because there was anything glorious about crucifixion, but because Jesus is awesome. We can despise crucifixion and still revel in Christ.

This is important to understand because Christians, far too often, do their best Ned Flanders impression by just turning their frowns upside down as to ignore reality. This creates a superficiality and triteness within the church. Someone was murdered. Well, he is in a better place. Someone was raped. Well, all things work together for good. Your house burns down. Well, He who began a good work in you and such. You've got cancer. Well, you can do all things through Christ, and so on.

When we come to the Scriptures, it is a terribly honest book. Every single person I can think of in the Scriptures suffered in some way. There is no superficiality contained in this book. There is no triteness contained in this book. Yet, when it comes to our own lives we feel as though we either have to ignore or deny the way things are in order to either justify God, or to prove that we've done nothing to deserve what's happening.

Another error that we can make is to only see the suck and not what it produces. This is to acknowledge the reality of the situation, but then struggle terribly with it; especially if circumstances are outside of your control, or if the depth of the suck continues to compound like Job's did. Embracing the suck means to not give up and to not give in. In times like this the temptation is to question God. Not good. Or, to grow bitter. Also, not good. This is where we look to Jesus, the Author and Perfector of our faith, remembering all that He unjustly endured and all that He accomplished.

So much of the Christian life is to keep your hands to the plow and to keep moving forward. But for plows to work they have to dig into the hard ground and encounter resistance, without this, there is no new growth, no new life. So, as you approach the day do so with joy and embrace the suck.

# Chapter Twenty Three

# Remember to Look Up

We like buying potential and then seeing it realized. However, the last home we bought was a real booger. And by booger, I mean dump with lots and lots of potential. However, before the potential will ever be realized, there is a ton of work that needs to be done. In fact, if you think about all the work that needs to get done at the same time your brain could explode.

Termites, cockroaches, foundation issues, black mold, cracked roof rafters, rotten sub-floor, pink siding which fortunately matches the pink toilets, leaky windows, and those are just a few of the more minor things. Before we could even begin working, we had weeks of demo and dumpster filling. Every project that we have started thus far, has led to another project that was hiding another project that was yet wrapped in another project – kind of like a Russian Doll with deeply embedded layers of crap.

In what we thought would be a quick win and would help to build some momentum, my wife and I decided to demo our half bath on our main floor. We figured the whole thing would only take about a week – big win, no problem. However, after ripping everything out we were able to see the subfloor which was rotten from water damage. After ripping out that layer of subfloor there was another layer of subfloor that was also rotten.

After ripping it all out and peering into our basement, while covered in sweat, dirt, blood and disappointment, I think my wife could sense just a wee bit of discouragement permeating from me. She said, "looks pretty bad." To which I responded with something upbeat and inspirational, like, "This sucks." She said, "Yeah, I guess you have to remember to look up."

When we started the half bath, we also had an unplanned replacement of the ceiling for reasons that escape my mind at the moment, but I do remember that it sucked pretty good as well. As I took my eyes off the hole in the floor that used to be our bathroom and the pile of rotten boards next to me, I looked up and saw a beautiful new piece of drywall overhead. Sometimes you just got to remember to look up.

Yeah, everything was a mess, but everything in life is a mess until it's not. Dominion is ordering chaos, it's fixing and restoring broken things, it's replacing the rot, it's cleaning up the mess. In short, dominion is a process. The Christian life is a process. Sanctification is a process. And often, perhaps more often than we care to admit, we're so focused on what's right in front of us that we forget to look up. We look at the mess, and in our exhaustion we think that's all there is. We forget that the mess is part of the process. We forget the progress already made. We forget the vision that got us started in the first place and we forget to look up.

The author of Hebrews says this,

> Therefore, since we are surrounded by so great a cloud of witnesses, let us also lay aside every weight, and sin which clings so closely, and let us run with endurance the race that is set before us, looking to Jesus, the founder and perfector of our faith, who for the joy that was set before him endured the cross, despising the shame, and is seated at the right hand of the throne of God. (Heb. 12:1-2)

112

Jesus endured the cross because of the joy that was set before Him. This doesn't mean that the cross was enjoyable in any way. The joy that was set before Him was everything that He was accomplishing through enduring the cross. Namely, the vindication of the Father's holiness and justice through His wrath being poured out on sin, and also the vindication of lost and broken sinners through the penal substitutionary death of Jesus in their place. At the cross, justice and mercy are on full display. At the cross we see what the Father is like in wrath and love.

Christ endured the cross with joy because through it, and His subsequent resurrection and ascension, He was seated at the right hand of the throne of God. He is renewing all things and building His church, which even the gates of hell cannot stop its advance in the world. Your life and my life are just little itty-bitty microcosms of God's redemption and restoration in the world.

Paul encouraged the Philippian church with these words, "And I am sure of this, that he who began a good work in you will bring it to completion at the day of Jesus Christ." (Phil. 1:6). Paul wrote those words from prison by the way. This process, this work, doesn't look like the evangelical pastor with his porcelain grill, freshly pressed suit and his glammed-out wife. More often than not, it looks like a big fat hot mess. It looks like holes in the floor and rotten wood all around.

Why is that? Because God is faithful to complete what He has started in you. God is remaking you in the image and likeness of His Son and there is a whole lot of junk that needs to be uprooted and removed. Often times that's painful, unpleasant, and uncomfortable, but it's all part of the process of beautifying a life.

Life can be very challenging and hard. This is good. On our way to the Celestial City there are rivers to cross and hills to climb. However, on our way, we can't forget to look up so that we don't lose our way.

## Chapter Twenty Four

# Keep Moving Forward

In, perhaps the greatest movie of all time, *Rocky Balboa,* Rocky delivers the greatest speech of all time. An over-aged Rocky is looking at getting back in the ring for an exhibition bout with the current heavyweight champion of the world. Rocky's son tells him not to do it. He tells him he is going to make a fool out of himself, with the unintended consequence of embarrassing him. Rocky tells his son how amazing he thinks his son is and how, when he was a baby, he would look at him and think about how he would grow up to be such an awesome person, but that something happened to him along the way. His son became entitled, while at the same time being afraid of making a name for himself and getting out of his father's shadow. Rocky then delivers the greatest lines in cinematic history...arguably...

Let me tell you something you already know. The world ain't all sunshine and rainbows. It's a very mean and nasty place and I don't care how tough you are it will beat you to your knees and keep you there permanently if you let it. You, me, or nobody is gonna hit as hard as life. But it ain't about how hard ya hit. It's about how hard you can get hit and keep moving forward. How much you can take and keep moving forward. That's how winning is done!

I have these words printed on a canvas with a picture of Rocky with his fists raised high at the top of the stairs at the Philadelphia Art Museum. The reason for this is because I want to be reminded of them daily. My wife and I actually use this expression, "keep moving forward," daily in our home. Probably, multiple times a day and applied to multiple situations. We use it with our children and their schoolwork, and their chores and their projects. No matter how hard it gets, keep moving forward. My wife and I use this expression in all areas of our life, but especially regarding our massive home renovation.

These words remind me of Winston Churchill's famous words, "Never give in, never give in, never, never, never, never – in nothing great or small, large or petty – never give in except to convictions of honor and good sense." There was a book that we used to read to our children when they were little called, *We're Going on a Bear Hunt*. Every obstacle the family would run into, they couldn't go over it and they couldn't go under it, and they couldn't go around it, they had to go through it.

Life, in just about every situation and in just about every way is the same. You just have to go through it, you have to keep moving forward. This is the only way something is completed. This is the only way something is overcome, through a continued progress in the same direction over time. This may sound silly, but we have also found these words very encouraging regarding home renovation projects.

As I write this, we are currently living in our biggest renovation yet. That is, my family of seven that shares our home with two bulldogs, four rabbits, two guinea pigs, and twenty chickens is living in an almost 6000 square foot renovation. When I say renovation, I mean the entirety of the house is currently tore up, meaning there has not been one square inch that hasn't been affected by demo in some way. With my family doing all of the demo, and all of the reno.

This means that there are a lot of things started with nothing finished. Given such a situation, I think you could easily see how this could quickly become overwhelming. And when I say overwhelming, I mean crying violently, wetting your pants while curled up in a corner eating a gallon of ice cream. Not that I have ever done that, that would be ridiculous. I am just saying, hypothetically, if someone were to do that, under those circumstances you would completely understand...right?

There are times where you feel like you're not moving forward no matter how hard you try. You don't even feel like you're just spinning your tires in place, but rather rolling backwards downhill, a very steep hill, in perhaps a very desolate mountainous region where you are alone and the hills are very, very steep. What do you do at that point? You keep moving forward. Every morning, after my wife and I debrief over coffee...lots of coffee, we always conclude with the words, "keep moving forward." No matter what's in front of us, or what the day may hit us with, there is only ever one option, you have to go through it. You keep moving forward.

The amazing thing is, if you keep your head down and your hands to the plow, no matter how big, how daunting, how overwhelming something may have seemed, you get through it. I find these words very encouraging and helpful not just regarding situations, circumstances, and projects that we face in life, but I also find them encouraging and helpful when applied to our walk with Christ. Perhaps there is no quicker summation of being a disciple than these simple words, keep moving forward.

Like that great theologian, Rocky Balboa said, "The world ain't all sunshine and rainbows. It's a very mean and nasty place and I don't care how tough you are it will beat you to your knees and keep you there permanently if you let it." Even just a short time in ministry will expose you to a tremendous amount of sin, and pain, and sorrow, and loss and tragedy, and that's just in the church. Life is filled with not only obstacles and seemingly impossible tasks, but also trials and tragedies that no one plans for, and nobody gets a hall pass. You're not getting over it, you're not getting under it, and you're not going around it. You have to go through it and the only way to do that is to keep moving forward.

The good news is that all of this is by design. God works according to the counsel of His will. He is the great Designer and Architect, and He is the great Renovator and Restorer of our souls. He disciplines those He loves as a father disciplines His children, and He often does so in ways that are not always apparent to the child. There are often things we don't understand, but this does not mean that God is taken aback by anything. God is using all of this to make us more like His Son, Jesus, in true knowledge, righteousness, and holiness.

James says, "Count it all joy, my brothers, when you meet trials of various kinds, for you know that the testing of your faith produces steadfastness. And let steadfastness have its full effect, that you may be perfect and complete, lacking in nothing." (James 1:2-4).

God is working all things together for good for those who love Him. We don't always get to choose what mountains we are going to climb in life. It's true, some of them we do, and others are just put in front us. It is also true, that life is filled with unknowns and uncertainties. However, here are a couple of things that I know for certain. You will never get over that mountain if you don't start moving, and you will never get to the other side if you don't keep moving forward. That's how winning is done.

# Chapter Twenty Five

# Function Before Beauty

I hate designers. Okay, well I don't hate all designers, and I don't necessarily hate designers in principle. I just hate *most* designers. In part, because I think they are usually one dimensional when they think through home renovation, and don't have a proper understanding of the household and the home in God's economy. Not only that, but when you employ a designer you're going to drop a lot more money on a project, kind of like creating another government agency. And they seem to spend money about as effectively as well.

Which is to say, that there often seems to be a lack of budget consciousness. But hey, it's other people's money so, who cares. At least at the end of the day, it always looks very pretty, most of the time. We've all seen the shows where they will spend like $10,000 on a bunk bed and climbing wall, or some type of princess themed room, and the kids are like ten years old and you know darn well, that's going to be cool for like a week, and in a couple years is going to be super dated. But the designers don't care because it looks awesome on their Instagram and for the show. We've also seen them buy the Cadillac tile for the kitchen at the expense of doing any other renovations on the rest of the home that the family desperately needs. We've even seen the shows where they are given an astronomical amount of money to renovate a home, like the same amount of money it would cost to rebuild it, and they still can't figure out how to stay in budget.

All of this kind of stuff drives me nuts because it just seems self-serving and actually shows a lack of creativity and, well, design. For example, the client wants a new kitchen layout, but the designer has it in their mind to use the budget on all high-end finishes, which usually amounts to them spending the client's money on a bunch of over-priced stuff so they can feel fancy. So instead of the layout changing in the kitchen, which would benefit the family the most and improve the function of their home the most, the layout stays the same because the designer chooses to spend the entire budget on beauty over function. This is absolutely stupid, like violently and painfully stupid. A good designer should be able to figure out both.

Proverbs 17:1 says, "Better is a dry morsel with quiet than a house full of feasting with strife." Let me rephrase it this way, it is far better to have a home that functions well than one that photographs better on Instagram and tickles the designer's ego.

The heart of what I believe is happening here is misplaced priority, coupled with a lack of holistic vision regarding the home. Far too many designers think their sole job is just to make things pretty. I don't think they would actually confess that much, but that's what I see happening far too often in reality. A good designer should mimic their heavenly Father who is the best Designer and Architect. This means that form and function and beauty should all be baked into the cake of whatever it is that we are working on, of course within budget...most of the time.

Being made in the image of God, we will naturally seek a balance between function and beauty within our homes. For example, if something functions well for us, but we think it's butt ugly, well then, we will naturally try to make it prettier. If something is pretty but does not function well or at all, we will naturally question it's use.

The way this all plays out in the home is a bit relative to each home. Namely, the vision that you have for your household, where you are at in life, your vocation, budget, available time, lifestyle, size of your family and so on. Based on all these factors and variables you then prioritize accordingly for your home, always seeking to leverage and stretch and maximize the impact of your budget.

Proper prioritization helps us to know what to spend where, and when and how in a way that fits within our lives. Having these priorities worked out can also help to reduce lots of frustration and anxiety that many people have regarding their homes. We can't have it all, but what we can do is order our lives and our homes according to our priorities and our resources so we can have what's most important to us. This should always put us in a place that majors in the majors and minors in the minors.

Proverbs 24:27 illustrates this perfectly, "Prepare your work outside; get everything ready for yourself in the field, and after that build your house." Some say that this is a general reminder to focus on the most important things in life and spend less time and energy on the less important things. Some say there is a lesson here, that we should spend time on how we are going to provide for a family before we have a family. Others say that this is a clear principle of majoring in the majors before minoring in the minors.

There is no doubt that this proverb, and every other, has a broad application, but the principle is clear, prioritize your life accordingly. For purposes of our discussion, this applies directly to our homes regarding function and beauty. The very foundation to this entire discussion is the vision that you have for your home, and your family.

If you are like most people, you are just busy living your life before you get busy thinking about *how* you are living your life. That is, more often than not, our lives are living us and we're not living them. Another way of saying this is that we simply get caught up living on the activity treadmill moving from one thing to the next. We often feel like a kite in a hurricane wondering who is holding the string. Ten years go by, twenty years go by, and we step back and ask ourselves, how in the world did that happen?

What do you want for your home? What do you want your marriage, family and work to look like? If you don't have a target you'll hit your mark every time. Like I said, most of us don't start out with this in mind. We just want to get married, own a home, do good work and make some babies. All of that is magnificent, but now what? What do you want your marriage to look like? What do you want your home to look like? What do you want your work to look like? And how is all of that blessing and shaping your children and others?

Regardless of where we're at, we start where we are at and work with what we got. God is awesome and this is exactly what He does with us in Christ - transforming, molding, shaping directing, and ordering our lives to His. Yes, and Amen. Through repentance and faith in Christ, we are a new creation, that is what we are. We should then function accordingly, and as we do our lives will become more and more beautiful. Who Christ is gives us a standard and a norm with which to conform our lives to. As we look to Him, and set our eyes upon Him, our lives will move towards that end.

It is very much the same in our homes, which makes complete sense because this is ground zero for our lives. First, we have to cast a vision and then prioritize that within our means. After doing so, we can then make anything prettier, but the pretty should always be secondary to the form and function. If a designer is simply designing a home based on what they think is pretty, then they are putting the cart way before the horse.

How can you best maximize the capacity of the gifts and abilities of everyone in your home and how does your home best facilitate that? Determine what is most important for your household and then prioritize everything towards that end. Not only will this help you to make everything beautiful, but there is a certain beauty in this in and of itself. "Prepare your work outside; get everything ready for yourself in the field, and after that build your house." (Prov. 24:27).

## Chapter Twenty Six

# Start Small and Keep at It

I really enjoy working on my home. I am not a particularly skilled craftsman, but what I lack in skill I make up for in desire and creativity. I think all men need a hobby and tinkering on my house just so happens to be one of mine. By God's grace this is something that my wife and I have always done together. When we bought our first home neither one of us had ever done any type of home improvement, not even painting.

Our first house needed work, but it seemed like a castle fit for a king at the time. When we purchased it the whole thing was white, every room. My wife suggested one day that we paint the living room. At the time it seemed like an impossible task, but we thought we would give it a shot. We went to the store and bought some cheap rollers, brushes and some masking tape, which was really stupid, but it was cheaper than the fancy painter's tape. We picked a color together and bought our paint which was a total splurge at the time. I think it was like twelve bucks for a gallon. This was long before Bidenomics.

Then we did it; we stretched that whole dang gallon to do our whole living room. I'm pretty confident that if I were to see our work today I would be more than just a little embarrassed. But at the time, we were pretty proud of ourselves. It felt like we had just painted the Sistine Chapel. I'm pretty confident that we invited everyone we knew at the time over to behold our glorious work. We were now painters, or so we told ourselves, but even more than that, we were both now hooked on working on our house.

What once seemed like an impossible task for only the skilled elite we had now done. Albeit, most likely…almost certainly, badly, but we still did it, and anything worth doing well is worth doing poorly to begin. Sometimes in life just beginning is the victory, which kind of sounds like something that should go on a cat poster, but it's totally true. You can't get anywhere if you don't start somewhere. The sorriest people in life are the ones who never start anything, all the while complaining about everything they haven't done.

We figured that if we painted one room then surely we could paint another and then another and then another. If we could paint our house, then surely we could try our hands at tiling, flooring, trim, doors and windows, and so on. All it takes is a willingness to try, and then starting. So many people get so paralyzed at the idea of starting because they are afraid of not doing something well. But this is stupid. Of course you're not going to do it well, you are just starting.

This is one of the reasons why children are so amazing. Before they get self-conscious and start caring about what other people think, or about how they may appear to others, they try anything and everything. Being around children is wonderful because they still see the world as a place of wonders. It's all the adults that tell you that you shouldn't do something or try something that suck. Often this isn't anything that resembles actual advice, it's just a way to assuage their own shortcomings, fears, and insecurities.

124

Starting anything or trying anything for the first time is always intimidating until you do it. Of course you are going to mess up along the way. That's all part of the process and no education is free. The first time we bought fancy tile, and by fancy I mean not the cheapest economy tile they sell, I did something really stupid. I mixed my grout too thick and didn't clean off my tile as I went. The grout set on our entire bathroom floor on our fancy new tile. My wife and I were up until four in the morning scrubbing it clean. The funny thing was, we used black grout, so our fingers were stained for almost two weeks. That wasn't cool but no education is free, and I just paid the price to learn how to grout – awesome. I haven't made that mistake since.

If there is something you want to do, just start small and then get after it. This is a lesson that doesn't just apply to house renovations, but to everything in life including your faith. One thing I know for certain is that you are never going to grow in your walk with Christ if you don't start walking. Yes, often times things seem hard and even impossible on the front end, until they aren't any more.

So many get discouraged looking at the lives of others. We think they have it all together and seem to be so strong in the Lord. First of all, stop comparing yourself to others because it will rob you of your joy. Second of all, nobody has it all together. There are those in Christ that are truly amazing, however, many people that you think have it all together are just good liars and often trainwrecks behind closed doors.

If you want a healthy prayer life start praying. If you want to read your Bible more, stop talking about it, pick it up and start reading. You're not going to read the whole thing in a day, just get started and then don't stop. Pretty soon it will be normal. We should never get discouraged looking at the lives of other saints. We should be super encouraged knowing that they had to start somewhere too, and we should praise God that He always takes people where they are at.

Of course you're not the Apostle Paul. You haven't studied as much as Paul, you haven't suffered as much as Paul, and you haven't sacrificed as much as Paul. But just because you're not Paul doesn't mean that you can't grow in your faith. Start small, making incremental changes in your life over a long period of time. Then you will be amazed at how much you can accomplish and how much change you can bring to your life and those around you.

# Chapter Twenty Seven

# Asking for Help

Nobody is an island. Nobody is omniscient. Nobody has an unlimited amount of skill and ability. As awesome as Oholiab and Bezalel were, God filled them with skill of every sort, they still weren't unlimited. They still could not do everything themselves. They still needed help. This is very important to remember regarding any type of home renovation. Some people are awesome and are gifted in so many ways when it comes to this, and I am certainly not one of them. However, I can watch, I can listen, and I can learn from the awesome people, and when necessary, I can ask for help.

There is a tender balance here. No man wants to be completely dependent upon others. However, the idea of being completely self-sufficient, though it may sound awesome, is really impossible. I think this is why it's hard for most guys to ask for help regarding anything, let alone, something that dudes should just be good at. Granted some people are just better at some things than others, but all skills are learned and honed.

I have to remind myself of this regularly. For whatever reason, I have a tendency to continually overestimate my level of abilities. I think that I am so naturally awesome, that I neither need to learn nor hone my skills. They have just been there since birth. We'll just call it the divine gifting of awesomeness. Teddy Roosevelt said, "When you are asked if you can do a job, tell them, 'Certainly, I can.' Then get busy and find out how to do it."

The sentiment expressed by Teddy here has served me well in life. However, there are times, perhaps a lot more of them than I care to admit, when I realized my divine gifting of awesomeness is not as naturally awesome as I think, and I am reminded that I am a mere mortal that needs lots of learning and honing. Did I say this has happened more than I care to admit? Well, it has, like a lot.

There has been a multitude of times where I have needed help moving stuff, tearing stuff out, or just finishing up a project. There have been times where I have gotten neck deep in a project and totally messed things up and didn't know how to fix it, or where I just flat-out didn't know how to do something. In all these cases I have had to eat a piece of humble pie, sometimes the whole pie, and ask for help.

Over the years, I have been blessed much by other men coming along side me and helping me with projects. Not only have I been blessed by that, but their willingness to share their time and skills with me has not only increased my skill set but also the value of my home. This is wonderful. Praise God for that. It would be an amazing thing if we could all pour into each other in such a way. I think we call this discipleship.

In order to make any of this possible, you have to be willing to ask for help. I think men bond best when working side by side on a project, but you have to be willing to do the work. No man appreciates a lazy ass, especially if he is helping him on his home. So, if you have someone that is willing and able to help on a project, learn all you can from them and then pass it on.

If you get to the point on a project where you hit the bricks and are too embarrassed to ask for help or are unwilling to ask for help, then you will never grow past the point you're at. You've capped, and if nothing changes then nothing changes. You're not omniscient – get over it. What is more important to you? Looking like you're self-sufficient, or eating a piece of humble pie so that you can learn and grow into a greater degree of self-sufficiency?

There are also times where things just need to be outsourced, either because of time or because of the particularity of the skill set needed. This is all well and good but do your due diligence. Just because someone has been in business for a long time, or just because they have a state license doesn't mean they are competent. You have to know the right people to ask for help and you have to know the right people to hire out. It's like Luther said, "This world with devil's filled…" There are a lot of awesome people out there, but there are also a lot of snakes. Perhaps, far more snakes.

All of this is very similar in the church, and our walk with one another as we seek to walk with Christ. There are a lot of things that we have to do on our own and figure out. The church is a corporate body, but you are responsible for your relationship with Christ. The first place where that will be evidenced is in the home. This is also the rawest and the realist place where it's evidenced as well. You can easily fool other people for an hour here and an hour there, but it's really hard to fool the people you live with into thinking you are far more capable than you are.

My point is, we should be seeking to grow in grace and knowledge and then be blessing those closest to us first. But you will hit the bricks in life, you will need counsel and you will need help working through things. There will be times where you have to eat a piece of humble pie and ask for wisdom, counsel and help. You should be praying for God to bring qualified people into your life to help, but you can't be whiny and entitled about it. The same principles apply, you have to be willing to work, and learn and get after it.

However, I would urge caution here as well. You would hope that would not be the case in the church, but it is. People are sinners and that doesn't change just because they are in the church. Over the years in ministry, I can honestly say that some of the best and most awesome people are in the church, but so too are some of the worst. Snakes will always find a way to slither in, and unfortunately those are always the ones that are most willing to give advice.

Today we think that transparency is good. It can be, but not in an unqualified way. A blanket transparency before everyone isn't helpful because there are people that will take advantage of you, just like the tradesman that is looking to rip you off. You need to look for help from the right people. People with character, skill, and experience. A buddy that is willing to help you with your plumbing problem but doesn't know anything about plumbing really isn't going to be much help to you, though the desire to help is nice.

So then, we need to be willing to ask for help at times. We are all limited in our capacities, skills and experiences. And you're not necessarily whining when asking for help. You're not looking to be a leech. Every church has those people, and everybody naturally avoids them over time. You are looking to learn and grow, and in so doing you will be a bigger blessing to those around you.

# Chapter Twenty Eight

# Silver Lining and Stuff...

My family has been experiencing a whole lot of changes as of late. A good many of these changes are what we would call, uncomfortable, but as we've discovered, not all discomfort is discomforting. That is to say, there has been a silver lining in all of our experiences. Or, if you will, it would be more appropriate to say that God is good and always knows what He is doing even if we don't.

For example, we bought a house that we knew would need renovation, but we did not know the extent of the renovation. Like, we knew it would be a full gut, but the extent and scope of the full "guttedness" we didn't anticipate. This has dramatically pushed back timelines and created a lot of discomfort, and what we will simply call, "oh crap" scenarios.

Now there are a couple of ways to look at said crappiness. First, this is crappy, and that's it. Second, this is crappy, however, God has put this crappiness on our shoulders because He wishes us to become, not just more reliant on Him – yes and always...but also more self-reliant and resourceful, leading us to develop more skills that we would have never developed otherwise. As the old saying goes, "Necessity is the mother of all invention." Although, I personally would prefer to not be in a constant state of necessity as of late, God has seen fit to make me necessarily uncomfortable.

Through this, God has not only required that skills be developed but that mental and spiritual fortitude be developed. God is good, although walking with Him is rarely comfortable. As soon as we moved in the demo began, and along with it so did all the development and discomfort. Demo is usually enjoyable on the front end, and often therapeutic. However, the size and scope of this demo took its toll leading us to uncover one problem after another with one seemingly being bigger than the next.

It can be crippling and overwhelming when projects become much bigger, more expensive, with massive time delays and are coupled with humbling realizations of skill deficiency. Although we have experienced all of that, the silver lining here is that we've been able to uncover much that would go undetected under normal circumstances, making our house healthier and safer than it otherwise would have been. This has also enabled, or forced, us to acquire skills we wouldn't have acquired otherwise, or to make connections and meet people that we wouldn't otherwise have met.

However, the uncovering of all the "crappery," has led to a restriction in sleeping arrangements. When I say restriction, I mean this has led to our children sleeping in the same room with my wife and myself for an indefinite period of time. As one can imagine, this could very easily lead one to be a bit cranky, or perhaps to despair over the meaning of life itself.

The silver lining here is that God has given us much isolated time with our children that we would have never had. It has led to much laughter and conversations late into the night that we would never have had otherwise. Is it an inconvenience? Certainly, in some ways, but it is also a tremendous blessing in others. Will we be thankful when these arrangements are over? Yep, but I trust we will all look back and be thankful, with the thankfulness being accompanied by a wee bit of laughter.

Another example of this silver lining, in the midst of the crazy, is that we have had no appliances for some time. That is certainly not the silver lining, however what it has necessitated and produced is. Take for example, the lack of having a dishwasher. Is having one a blessing? You bet. However, it is also a blessing to see my wife and daughters do the dishes together at the end of the day, usually taking much longer than it needs to because they are chatting and laughing the whole time. This was something on the front end that was forced out of necessity, but now is something that they get to do together and has turned into a real blessing. Will we get a dishwasher in the future? Certainly, and as soon as we can. However, we will always look back on these moments with gratitude.

Here is just one more example out of a great multitude...well myriads upon myriads. Before we purchased this home out of state, we were told there was fiber internet in our area. This was necessary for us because we had plans of expanding *The Godly Troublemaker Podcast*, with our home being the home base of operations. Come to find out, after arriving, not only do we not, not have fiber internet, the only type of internet available in our area is worse than dial-up – just kidding, but not really. It is really that freakishly bad. This has put a halt on, or at least severely slowed down a lot of things that we had planned, which we are still trying to figure out and work around.

However, with this forced slow down, and full removal in some cases, the Lord has revealed to us just how much time we all waste online every day. Although this has been the source of a lot of frustration, this gift of time has also been a great blessing to my family. It has enabled us to accomplish other things and invest our time elsewhere and has also granted us more time together.

These may all seem like trite and little things, and perhaps in the grand scheme of things they are. However, God in His grace has answered many of our prayers through a multitude of things that have caused lots of uncomfortable circumstances. His mercies truly are new each morning. Not because He removes our discomfort, but rather because He blesses us and smiles at us through it.

# Chapter Twenty Nine

# Tomorrow is a New Day

In the 2000 film, *Castaway*, Tom Hanks plays Chuck Noland, a FedEx systems analyst and executive. He is a type A, driven personality as depicted by the classic line, "We live or we die by the clock. We never turn our back on it, and we never ever allow ourselves the sin of losing track of time." He finds himself stranded and alone on a deserted island as the only survivor of a plane crash. He somehow managed to survive all alone on the island for four years, before building a raft and rolling the dice by going out to sea. Miraculously, a cargo ship finds him adrift.

As he arrives home, it's not really the home that he left. He had been gone for four years and everyone believed he was dead, with the accompanying funeral and all. His fiancé is now happily married to another man, and they have children together. Chuck has somehow found his way back home, but he is just as lost as ever. He fought for his survival on that island and struggled to find his way back home, but the home he returned to is not the home he left. That which gave him a reason to live for four years wasn't there anymore. Now what?

Realizing his fiancé has moved on and reflecting upon all of this with his best friend, Chuck utters these words, "And I've lost her all over again. I'm so sad that I don't have Kelly. But I'm so grateful that she was with me on that island. And I know what I have to do now. I gotta keep breathing. Because tomorrow the sun will rise. Who knows what the tide could bring?"

Castaway is very much a story of survival and perseverance and hope. However, it is also very much a story about time and what matters most to us, and the desire inside all of us to find our way home. Many of us feel like Chuck Noland, living and dying by the clock, which is why so many of us long for our homes to be places of peace and rest. One of the interesting ironies of the film is that when Noland was stuck on the island, he was most free. He had been blessed with so much, but his life was completely out of whack, and he was a slave to the clock. I think that is a sentiment that most of us can understand. Psalm 90:12 says, "So teach us to number our days that we may get a heart of wisdom."

Our lives are generally busy and often chaotic, or at least they feel like it. For many, we work on our homes or embark on renovations of varying sizes and to varying degrees because we want our homes to be places of peace and rest, places filled with joy and free from the crazy and the chaotic. We hope that renovations will help bring peace and efficiency to our homes. That's usually the desire anyway. Because of this, starting is usually exciting, but rarely is the whole process as equally exciting.

We enter into a project like Chuck Noland, living and dying by the clock and ready to get 'er done. Somewhere along the way we crash and burnout. We feel like the only survivor stuck on an island that we can't get off of and we are just doing everything in our power to survive, telling ourselves, "To just keep breathing." Ok, maybe I am being a little dramatic, but it can feel that way at times.

Just a few weeks ago we had all our windows replaced. Forty-three custom sized windows that we didn't know we were going to need to replace when we purchased the home. Just F.Y.I. that was a real nut punch. As it turns out, the installers didn't take the time to let us know that the framing around one of the windows was rotten so that we could fix it, and more importantly so we could find the source of the water that was causing said rottenness. So, they just put a beautiful new window over a bunch of rotten wood and called it good. Not that I want to draw unwanted attention to this company, so I won't tell you that their name definitely doesn't rhyme with Home Depot.

Anyway, we would have been none the wiser until we got a heavy rain, which happens where we live. In fact, we get rain so hard that it would make Noah nervous. Anyway, the heavy rains came and so too did the water from the top of my window trim. Seeing this to be a most peculiar thing I took a closer look. As I looked closer, I was able to poke my finger all the way through the trim and rip the top casing trim out with my hand. There was so much water damage the wood was completely rotten. Again, this definitely wasn't Home Depot because they have professional installers.

Stuff like this absolutely sucks, but it's par for the course with renovations, and the bigger the renovation the more of this crap you will repeatedly have to deal with. It's generally not any one thing that breaks you but the cumulative effect of all of it. What do you do? Well, first just remember to breath. That's a good start. As I write this, I am literally watching water come in my house through this rotten sill surrounding this beautiful new window.

What am I going to do? I don't know yet. I don't even know how extensive the damage is, but I know it's not good. However, this isn't our first rodeo. All of this sucks and it's certainly not pleasant to watch, but we will get it fixed. No matter what happens, no matter how big the speed bump or how big the setback, tomorrow is a new day. In the absolute worst of circumstances, the prophet Jeremiah could write these words, "The steadfast love of the LORD never ceases; his mercies never come to an end; they are new every morning; great is your faithfulness. 'The LORD is my portion,' says my soul, 'therefore I will hope in him.'" (Lam. 3:22-24).

Regardless of how much today sucks, God's mercies are sufficient for the day. He is fully aware of everything that you are experiencing and going through and His steadfast love never ceases and His mercies never end. Regardless of what you may be going through today, tomorrow is a new day and the sun will rise.

No matter how big the suck, how big the setback, how big of a hit to the budget, no matter how much time it consumes, tomorrow is a new day. Just remember to breathe, the sun is going to come up and who knows what the tide may bring in.

# Chapter Thirty

# Maintenance

I heard someone say a while back that it is far easier to stay in shape than to get in shape. As a general principle this makes sense. If diet and exercise are already a normal part of your life that is certainly easier than adding it to your life. Already having a habit developed is much easier than developing one or making it a regular part of your schedule.

Another way of saying this, is that the maintaining of something built is easier than building it. No doubt there is still labor involved, but building is different than maintaining. Building or repairing an engine is much different from regular diagnostic tests and making sure all your fluids are capped off and fresh and so on.

However, even though it's easier, we often neglect regular maintenance. There is usually nothing romantic or fun about it. It's just tedious. You're not creating something new. You're just making sure that what you already have continues to function properly.

This means that even if something looks fine, you have to consider the normal wear and tear that is taking place. Every chiropractor or physical therapist that I have ever been to has told me the same thing. The best time to come in is before you are in extreme pain, and they even have the audacity to say that regular visits can prevent extreme pain.

Life is never a one and done. Everything under the sun breaks down, and nothing lasts forever. This means that things need to be replaced and maintained. We understand this when it comes to our bodies. We wish it wasn't so. It would be nice to workout hard and get in great shape and then be in shape for the rest of our life without any additional work required. That would be awesome and a total time saver, but that's not the way anything works and that's not the way it works in our homes either.

Renovating a home is a ton of hard work. It is fun, but it is also exhausting, and when you're done, you want to be done. I often sarcastically joke around with my wife by saying, "The only thing I enjoy more than doing a project once, is doing it twice." No one wants to go back and redo a project you just put a bunch of time and money into, but sometimes that's what you have to do if you want it done right.

The last house we were in had a bunch of big fellowship spaces which was great for Bible studies. We would have dinner and a study on Friday nights. Our house was always packed, and it wasn't uncommon to have twenty kids running around our house at any one time. Every Saturday afternoon I would go through our house that we just remodeled and patch and paint and repair what was dented, scuffed up or broken from the night before.

It didn't take us long to figure out that such a great pack of little sinners needed a greater degree of supervision, but even then, with that number of little ones it is like herding cats. So regardless, something was always getting jacked up. I could have just let all the little things go and wait until they added up. However, when we do this, projects seem to grow with compound interest, so we put them off because fixing everything will require more time, and then we never get around to it.

I think this is the case with a lot of people. They just let things go, and when you compound that over several years it can really devalue your home, because of the work that will be required to get it back in shape, so to speak. This is not as uncommon as you would think. People build a home, or have their home renovated and then never keep it up. This was the case with the last three homes we purchased, none of them had really been touched since they were built, and all of them showed the signs of wear, some worse than others.

Even though we believed these houses had a bunch of potential, they photographed terribly because they were ugly, and when I say ugly I mean ugly, not just take the glasses off the pretty girl ugly, but really ugly. Not surprisingly, this scares off a lot of potential buyers. This is the type of situation my wife and I love, because we know we should be able to get the house for a price that we think is a good value, and with a ton of work the house could be brought back to life. And if we decided to, we could sell it for a profit.

Because the previous owners neglected their homes, it was our gain. No one is going to pay a premium for a ton of work that they are going to have to do, and we were able to capitalize on that. It should be noted and understood that all of that could have been prevented with regular work and care and watchfulness. It's like the old saying, "An ounce of prevention is worth a pound of cure."

When we don't do this, things can get away from us and get away from us quickly. The leak that would have cost two hundred dollars to fix is now going to cost two thousand dollars because of the extemporaneous damage. This is also true regarding our physical health. A skip day here and a cheat day there doesn't seem like that big of a deal. Same thing with one pound here and one pound there. It's just one pound, but it's one pound repeatedly over an elongated period of time. Pretty soon you're asking yourself where that additional twenty pounds came from.

This is also true regarding our souls. It is not as though we ever arrive. It's true, we want to grow in knowledge, righteousness, and holiness. We want to manifest the presence of Christ in ourselves through the fruits of the Spirit and so on, but this is something we grow in and never really arrive at. Our lives are continual work and require continual maintenance. This is why regular Bible reading and prayer and worship and fellowship, and so on are so important. Assuming those things are taking place we are still told repeatedly in the Scriptures to be watchful. Here are just a few verses to keep in mind:

> Until I come, devote yourself to the public reading of Scripture, to exhortation, to teaching. Do not neglect the gift you have, which was given you by prophecy when the council of elders laid their hands on you. Practice these things, immerse yourself in them, so that all may see your progress. Keep a close watch on yourself and on the teaching. Persist in this, for by so doing you will save both yourself and your hearers. (1 Tim. 4:13-16)

> Be watchful, stand firm in the faith, act like men, be strong. Let all that you do be done in love. (1 Cor. 16:13)

> Continue steadfastly in prayer, being watchful in it with thanksgiving. (Col.4:2)

> Be sober-minded; be watchful. Your adversary the devil prowls around like a roaring lion, seeking someone to devour. (1 Pet. 5:8)

Watchfulness is so important because it's usually the little things, over extended periods of time, that turn into big problems that could have easily been avoided. It's been said that you get what you tolerate. This is true. But it is also true that what you tolerate today is coming back with compound interest tomorrow.

Therefore, be watchful over your soul and ever mindful of your walk with Christ. If we can understand this regarding our health and our home, how much more so should we be diligent regarding our souls?

## Epilogue

# Never Finished

D o you ever listen to music when you work on projects? I do. My song choices are pretty eclectic. Often times I'll start with the *Rocky III* theme song, rocking out "Eye of the Tiger." I'm not kidding. Sometimes that's what it takes to get me going on a project. Sometimes we'll belt out some 80's music, which my daughters love. They call them oldies, which I think is hilarious but also sad. I often let them know that the songs aren't as cool if you had to grow up with them, but I'm coming around. Sometimes it's country…most of the time it's country, but it seems like lately, the one song that is consistently played is Metallica's, "Nothing Else Matters."

Perhaps it's because the opening line in the song seems to describe our life to a tee, "So close no matter how far," pretty much sums it up. Always working, ever grinding trying to complete one project so that you can move to the next and then to the next and so on. Then, if by some miraculous event everything is brought to completion, you're on to the next thing.

It's a sensitive dynamic to balance, especially regarding renovation projects. The whole reason you embark down the laborious road of renovation is to create something more functional and more beautiful for your family. The reason we drive down any road is to get to our destination. The end is why we begin. The end is why we strive the way we do. We would never endure the inconvenience and discomfort and sacrifice without that. No one wants to suffer for suffering's sake. The last thing that most people want is to be stuck in a never-ending state of renovations…always working, always striving, never arriving. Perspective is helpful here.

The idea is to always complete the project but, in all honesty, you never really complete the project because ultimately it was never really about brick and mortar. In some respects, the work on our homes is never really done because things break down, things need to be replaced, and updated and so on. Needs change depending on the stage of life that we are in, and as a result our homes should reflect that. So, in that respect, our homes are always a work in progress because our lives are a work in progress.

This is what we need to keep in mind regarding renovations and projects, or new construction, or moving or whatever. None of these things are ends in and of themselves. The desire is always to go further up and further in, constantly looking to put God's fingerprints all over everything. We want our homes to give off a pleasing aroma to the Lord. In another respect, the work on our homes never ends because the work on our souls never ends. All the work is a means to this end.

The real beauty, the real craftsmanship, and real glory of any home is in the image bearers that fill it. We see this in the tabernacle and later in the temple, when the story of creation, fall and redemption is told through the construction and the tapestry and ornaments that filled it, culminating with the Holy of Holies, the Ark of the Covenant, and the Mercy Seat. That much is wonderful, but the reason why those places were so revered was because of the God who encountered His people there. He is all together holy. He is all together powerful. He is all together beautiful. Those places had weight because He is all together weighty.

By grace, through faith in Christ, you have been saved. You are a new creation, a dwelling for the Holy Spirit. I am not taking anything away from the church, and I am certainly not minimizing the gathered assembly of the saints, however the brick-and-mortar buildings that are owned by the saints are not the tabernacle or the temple. We are. We are the dwelling of the Holy Spirit. We are the hands and feet of Christ in the world. We are ambassadors of Christ, imploring the world to be reconciled to God through Christ. Therefore, the greatest ministry any of us will ever have is in our homes.

There is something very special about our gathered assemblies on the Lord's Day, and all the work that is performed by the church inside and outside of their buildings. Again, I am not minimizing any of that work. However, I am highlighting that just as we should see something special about the church, we should also see our homes as very special places, in fact even more so than our churches. There are some who may not understand that, but the reason the church is such a hot mess today is because people's homes are such a hot mess today. One is a reflection of the other and not visa-versa. The greatest, most impactful, and longest lasting generational effect of ministry happens within our homes.

Therefore, any work that may or may not be done on our homes is done with that in mind. Any renovations, any building, or moving should be done with that in mind. The thing that makes a dwelling a home are the ones that fill it. I tell my children, maybe not every day, but certainly multiple times a week, "You are my home." As long as I have my wife and kids with me, I don't really care where you put me. And wherever that may be, I'll be busy trying to make that a place where everyone can thrive.

Honestly, as I write this, I have about seven projects staring me in the face, and in many respects, at least externally, our lives have never been this big of a mess; and yet our home has never been filled with more laughter and joy and creativity. Sure, the work we are currently doing is being done with the hopes of facilitating more of that, and hopefully creating an environment that makes us all better in a great multitude of ways. However, when the projects are complete that doesn't mean that the work ends. The real work never ends, and in many respects, it will be just beginning, or perhaps hopefully continuing with more gusto.

My home will never make it in a magazine, nor be spoken of with any regard among man, however, that's not the goal. The goal is that it would be spoken of in heaven. I don't just want my home to be a little outpost and armory, I want it to be a little sanctuary – one filled with laughter and joy and creativity...and more laughter.

I know this is usually not the way people think about their homes and certainly not the way they think about home renovations. However, I hope this little book has changed that in your minds. If I could forever renovate the way we think of renovations by getting us to think of them through Christ, for Christ, in Christ, and by Christ I would be well pleased. Plus, walking in step with the masses is never really all that fun. Well-worn roads are smooth on the feet but taking the one less traveled makes all the difference.

Made in the USA
Columbia, SC
19 June 2024